Captain Wheeler

The Track of Fire

Or, A Cruise with the Pirate Semmes

Captain Wheeler

The Track of Fire
Or, A Cruise with the Pirate Semmes

ISBN/EAN: 9783337052737

Printed in Europe, USA, Canada, Australia, Japan

Cover: Foto ©ninafisch / pixelio.de

More available books at **www.hansebooks.com**

No. 5. No. 5.

IRWIN P. BEADLE'S TEN CENT NOVELS

The Ocean Cloud in Flames.

THE TRACK OF FIRE.

NEW YORK:
IRWIN P. BEADLE & CO'S
TEN CENT PUBLISHING HOUSE FOR THE MILLION.

W. D. Baker, Cleveland, O.

Entered, according to Act of Congress, in the year 1864, by IRWIN P. BEADLE & ... the Clerk's Office of the District Court of the United States for the Southern Dis... New York.

THE MAN-EATERS;
OR,
The Cannibal Queen

DESCRIPTION OF THE QUEEN KALOTA.

She was about twenty-two years of age, above the medium he... and possessed a stately step, and a form as straight as the palm t... that shaded her isle. Her complexion was a dark olive; her ... black and small, though piercing in their glances, and shining w... an unvarying, diamond-like lustre. Her cheeks were stained a l... red, as was her large neck and shoulders, and her full, naked bos... Her hair was long, bushy, and frizzled, and arranged grotesq... with ribbons and shells. The lobes of her ears were enormo... distended with holes, in which were suspended an immense pai... ear-rings. The expression of her countenance was repulsive, ... indicative of strong animal passions. Her dress was a compro... between the simplicity of the native Feejeean costume and the ... ropean attire, being composed of a short silk skirt, of a bright s... let hue, edged with a heavy silken fringe which fell to her b... knees; a pair of gaily embroidered shoes, and a loose open jack... which revealed, rather than concealed, the upper half of her pers...

"What you say to-day, Capt. Linn?" asked Kalota, in very tol... able English, she having learned a good deal of the language fro... the missionary, in order to render herself more agreeable to her c... durate captive.

"The same as before and always," replied the captain.

A scowl passed over the queen's face, but she instantly assumed ... smile meant to be tender and persuasive, and approached him.

"I make you one more offer," she said, putting her arms aroun... him and caressing him. "I make you king, and you be my husban... I love you, and give you everything you want—eh, Capt. Linn?"

The eager, rapturous expression on her countenance disgusted o... hero, and he freed himself from her encircling arms, saying:

"You had better go home, Kalota, and marry one of your ow... kind. I have got some one else to love me, and I love her. I ca... not marry you."

A look of fiendish jealousy appeared on the face of the savag... beauty, and she said:

"Ah! you love 'nother woman! Is she pretty as me?"

Man-Eaters will be issued Feb. 15th, 1864.

IRWIN P. BEADLE & Co.,
PUBLISHERS,
37 William Street, New York.

THE TRACK OF FIRE;

or,

A Cruise with the Pirate Semmes.

A CHRONICLE OF STARTLING ADVENTURES ON THE OCEAN.

By CAPTAIN WHEELER, U. S. A.

Author of "THE WEB OF FATE," "RUNNING THE BLOCKADE,"
"THE SECRET DESTROYER,"
&c., &c.,

NEW YORK:
IRWIN P. BEADLE & CO., PUBLISHERS,
137 WILLIAM STREET.

Entered according to Act of Congress, in the year 1863,

By IRWIN P. BEADLE & CO.

In the Clerk's Office of the District Court of the United States
for the Southern District of New York

T. R. DAWLEY, ELECTROTYPER, 13 PARK ROW, N. Y.

THE TRACK OF FIRE.

CHAPTER I.

CAPT. SEMMES AND HIS LIEUTENANT—THE BURNING SHIP—THE "ALABAMA" AWAITING HER PREY!

Late one pleasant evening, about the middle of September, 1863, the famous piratical cruiser *Alabama* was lying in Table Bay, in front of Cape Town, thirty miles north of the Cape of Good Hope. Her commander, Capt. Raphael Semmes was leaning over her bulwarks, on the inshore side, looking towards the town and peaks of Table Mountain, which rise so precipitously above it. The history of Capt. Semmes, his personal characteristics, etc., are too well known to the world at large to require mention in these pages.

"Lieutenant Murlick," he said, suddenly turning to an officer passing near him, "when shall we make that little trip ashore? To-night?"

"If you think best, Capt. Semmes," replied the person addressed, as he paused beside his superior. "If the Fed's hunt us through the Indian ocean, as they have hunted us in the Atlantic, we had certainly better have the specie safely stowed away behind us."

"Just so! Get out a boat, and come to the cabin, and we'll set about it. We will not take any of the men with us!"

Lieut. Murlick hastened to comply with this order.

He was one of the most villainous-looking men it is possible to imagine.

He was about forty-five years of age, with grizzly hair and beard, with front teeth showing like a rat's, with small and twinkling eyes, which were full of cold-blooded selfishness and cruelty, and his visage was characterized by the most evil and repulsive expressions.

Nature had originally written villian on his countenance, and every event of his life had set this seal deeper and deeper upon it.

"That will do, boys," he said, after a couple of seamen had lowered a boat by his orders. "You can go. The captain and I are merely going to take a little row by ourselves on the bay!"

He fastened the boat under the steamers quarter, and entered the cabin. The watch on deck paid but little attention to these proceedings, and the officers and men off duty had mostly turned in, leaving the cabin to the two confederates.

"There are four of the boxes, Murlick," said Semmes, who was bringing out some small iron chests, with handles, from his state-room—"two for you, and two for me. We shall want a couple of spades, and it may be well to take a dark lantern!"

The iron chests, which appeared to be very heavy, were placed in the boat, and the two men were soon rowing leisurely towards the northern side of the bay.

The two chests belonging to Capt. Semmes contained gold.

The contents of the other two were chiefly silver.

This money had been saved by the two men from the captures of specie they had made in the *Alabama*.

With a wise prevoyance, they had resolved on placing it where it would not be exposed to the hazards of war.

"We can't be expected to risk our lives for nothing, Murlick," observed Capt. Semmes when the boat was out of hearing from the steamer. "If the Confederacy becomes a fixed fact, she will not need this money. If she fails, *we* cannot very well get along without it!"

Murlick muttered his assent to these views.

"I hope I have been liberal with you added, Semmes—"giving you twenty thousand dollars of this secret fund, and reserving to myself forty thousand. I believe that's about the lion's share," and he laughed. "I think that we have managed the whole affair so that our brother officers do not suspect us. As to the men, they've had no chance, of course, to see what we are doing!"

Thus conversing, the two men reached the shore of a lonely creek shaded by thick bushes, and stunted trees, in a retired part of the bay, on the northern side, three miles from the town.

They went ashore, looking around, and came to the conclusion, that no one beside themselves was stirring in that region, all being still.

It was now near midnight.

The brilliant moon-light and star-light—the quiet waters of the bay—the heights of the neighboring mountains—the sleeping town—the solitude of the shore near them—all the features of the scene were full of a weird tropical beauty.

"Of course, we have every faith in each other," remarked Semmes, as he landed.

"Of course—of course!"

"At the same time, each had better keep his own secret. Thus, while I go westward along the shore, with my two boxes of specie. You may go eastward with yours—there's a shovel apiece—you can bury yours at any place you may select after getting out of my sight, and I will do the same with mine. In thirty minutes more or less, we will meet at this spot!"

Murlick again muttered his assent, and the two men separated, each going his appointed way, and taking a spade and his chests of money with him. Semmes was the first to return to the boat, but was speedily joined by his lieutenant.

"In this way," said Semmes, "we shall have no fears nor apprehensions of each other, let what will happen. You do not know where I have buried my money, nor do I know where you have buried yours. And now that the job is off our hands we will breathe more freely!"

They seated themselves in the boat and pushed off, returning to the steamer.

"We have made the Cape our head-quarters long enough," observed Semmes to Murlick, when they were again at their ease in the cabin of the *Alabama*. "It has doubtless been generally reported to the federal cruisers where we are. We must go up to the Bay of Bengal. Between here and there, if fortune favors me, I will destroy every United States vessel we may encounter. Every night shall witness a grand ship-burning. The East-Indian route shall be a perfect *track of fire*, illuminated by the conflagration of the ships we capture!"

"Good. I approve of a general destruction. It's sheer folly to take bonds from vessels, and let them go. The collection of those bonds is too many generations distant. The true way is to sink, burn and destroy!"

An hour later, the *Alabama* was standing out of Table Bay, headed towards the Cape, on her way to the East-Indian waters.

The following forenoon, when off Algoa Bay, she captured an East-Indiaman, the *Ceres*, of Boston, homeward bound with a valuable cargo.

Several other vessels were boarded during the day, but they proved to be English or French, and were not molested.

When the shades of night had again enveloped the scene, the steamer was hove to, and the *Ceres* fired, as a *decoy* to any merchantmen which might be sailing in those waters. Semmes had saved her until this hour for this purpose, in accordance with his usual *modus operandi*.

As the flames, kindled in the cabin and hold of the doomed ship, reached the deck, and commenced climbing the masts and shrouds, the *Alabama* withdrew beyond the glare of the conflagration, and became motionless on the water.

Grim and silent as well as threatening, she lay just without the circle illuminated by the burning ship, and waited and watched for her prey!

CHAPTER II.

FALLING INTO THE TRAP.

The *decoy* ship of Capt. Semmes had not been vainly lighted.

Within a few leagues of the meridian reached by the *Alabama*, a stately clipper-ship was standing eastward, with a gentle breeze, and all her sails drawing.

She was the *Ocean Cloud*, of Boston, homeward bound, with a cargo of hemp, indigo, coffee and pepper.

On the deck of the vessel, looking thoughtfully out upon the sea, stood a gentleman, whose bearing was at once commanding and prepossessing—Mr. Jacob Vale, for many years a prominent merchant of Boston.

He was the owner of the vessel.

He had lately retired from active business, afflicted with ill-health, brought upon him by too close application to his multitudinous affairs, and his physician had recommended a sea-voyage, which he had accordingly taken.

The expression of Mr. Vale's face was sadly thoughtful, and he frequently sighed.

"Twenty years ago to-night, since my poor boy disappeared," he at length ejaculated, half unconsciously. "Is he yet living? Shall I ever see him?"

A young lady came out of the cabin, and put her arm through Mr. Vale's, saying:

"Dear father, you slipped away from me unnoticed!"

As indicated by her words, she was the daughter of the retired merchant. Her name was Ethel. She was about eighteen years of age, gentle and unaffected, with a remarkably well-balanced character, a rare degree of intelligence, and a cultivated mind. Her eyes were dark, and beamed with spirit and tenderness, her complexion was of a pale brunette tint, and her lips were red like coral. She was graceful and winning, and was as lovely in her disposition as in person.

"I thought you wouldn't be lonely in the society of Capt. Willis," replied Mr. Vale, pressing the radient girl to his heart. "You and he seem to be very attractive to each other."

The girl blushed and looked over the side of the vessel, concealing her face from her father.

"Besides," added Mr. Vale, "my thoughts have been much occupied to-day with your lost brother. Strange that thoughts of him have come over me so often lately! Can it be that he lives, and that our fates are to be in some way re-united?"

"Tell me all about him, dear father," said Ethel, after a pause. "You have never yet told me the particulars of his disappearance, the subject being so hopeless and painful."

Mr. Vale caressed his daughter a moment in silence, and then said:

"Since he is frequently in my thoughts, and not as one dead, I will tell you the story. In 1842, your mother and I were married, while I was yet a clerk. During our courtship, your mother had been much persecuted and annoyed by the attentions of a suitor named Abner Murlick, a clerk in a rival house. This person uttered fearful threats against us both before and after our marriage, but suddenly left the city, and we incidentally learned that he had gone to New Orleans. Three years after, our first-born son was taken from his little wagon, one day, when he was out with his nurse for an airing. She stood on the common, looking at some passing show, and when she turned the boy had vanished. We suspected that Murlick had abducted him, but all our subsequent efforts to find either Eugene or his supposed abductor were fruitless!"

As Mr. Vale ended this brief narration, Capt. Willis came on deck. He was about twenty-five years of age, tall and slender, with an originally fair complexion now browned by exposure to wind and sun; with light blue eyes, honest and expressive in their glances; with light brown hair waving carelessly over his high broad forehead; and with a general appearance at once noble and distinguished. He had been a poor boy, without a friend in the world, but had supported and educated himself, attaining a high degree of mental cultivation, and had adopted the sea as his profession, eventually reaching his present position of commander and part owner of the clipper.

"A fine night, Mr. Vale," he remarked, "and we are making fair progress in the direction of home!"

"Yes," replied Mr. Vale, making room for the young Captain at his side, "and if we do not see any of the Confederate rascals who are turning their attention to this quarter, we will soon be on the other side of the line!"

The manner of Mr. Vale showed that he regarded Capt. Willis with the utmost respect and esteem. The girl's silent reception of him was still more flattering, the color coming and going in her clear cheeks, and her eyes sparkling with an appreciative light. It was clear that while Mr. Vale and our hero were firm friends, the daughter and the young commander were lovers.

The question of meeting Confederate pirates was discussed in all its bearings, and Mr. Vale then withdrew to the cabin, telling Ethel not to remain too long in the evening air.

Arm in arm, the young couple strolled up and down the deck, Ethel inquiring the probable depth of the ocean at that point, the distance to the nearest land, the length of a voyage between the Cape of Good Hope and Boston, etc. Together they watched the moon-light playing on the waves, the flight of the sea-gulls, and the dashing of the billows.

Say what they would, however, it was evident that they had not yet given full expression to the emotions of their souls.

The truth was, they were only just awakening to the fact that they were all the world to each other.

They had known each other for years—ever since our hero had shipped as a cabin-boy on one of Mr. Vale's vessels—but it was only since the commencement of the present voyage that they had become intimately acquainted with each other.

"Do you ever think of the past, Ethel?" asked Capt. Willis, after a somewhat awkward pause, during which he seemed to be schooling some deep emotion. "Do you remember when I was a cabin-boy, and Capt. Brown used to send me with messages to your father, and you used to talk so kindly to me and wish that you could be a sailor? Notwithstanding the years that have passed since then, I recollect all those events as freshly as if they were of yesterday."

"And so do I!" responded Ethel, warmly. "Those days often recur to me. I remember that, on one of these visits, when I was studying a difficult French lesson, you assisted me, to father's great surprise. It was that ability that first determined him to look after your advancement."

"Your father has been very kind to me, Ethel——"

"That is because you have been very deserving, Edward,," she quickly replied. "Father merely recognized your merit!"

The honest face of Capt. Willis betrayed the effect of these kind assurances upon him. He looked tenderly at his companion, drawing her nearer to him, and seemed about to make a declaration of his love to her, when a light suddenly flashed upon her sight, from a point at a great distance, almost directly in his course.

"What can it be? A signal, or a burning ship?" asked the girl.

Capt. Willis looked anxious.

"It looks like a burning ship," he replied. Excuse me a moment. I will get my glass and call Mr. Vale!"

The merchant was soon regarding the phenomenon, and exchanging speculations with Capt. Willis and Ethel, all considerably excited.

The glass revealed nothing at first, but ere long distinctly, as the flames grew larger, and the ship drew nearer to it, Capt. Willis perceived that the light was occasioned by the burning of a ship, the masts and rigging being revealed in a sheet of fire.

He exchanged anxious glances with Mr. Vale, observing:
"That looks like the presence of our enemies!"

Mr. Vale looked through the glass a moment, and then said,
"Clearly, a ship is on fire. It may be a decoy or not. Capt. Semmes, of the *Alabama*, is reported to be in this vicinity, and it may be that this is one of his traps to catch us!"

An earnest consultation followed, in which Ethel took part. The question to be decided was whether to approach the burning ship or not.

"The case stands like this," finally said Mr. Vale. "If the burning ship is an honest trader, we ought to go to her relief. If the thing is a Confederate trap, and we lose our vessel, why, I can afford it. I mean by this that I had rather take the risk of this loss than the risk of neglecting a score or more of perishing fellow-creatures in their extremity!"

Capt. Willis and Ethel both approved of this generous decision, and the former gave orders for the ship to be kept away towards the scene of disaster.

"I see nothing of any second vessel—of any steamer in waiting," proceeded Mr. Vale, after a long and anxious discussion of the whole subject. "At the worst, if we fall into the hands of the pirates, they'll send us ashore at the Cape or elsewhere, and our misfortunes will be chiefly felt in my pockets. On the whole, we'll proceed to the scene of trouble!"

The noble clipper rapidly shortened the distance between her and the burning vessel. Her crew prepared to launch the boats, collected ropes, and made other dispositions that seemed likely to be useful. She was at length sufficiently near to the conflagration for Mr. Vale and Capt. Willis to take the alarm—to see that there was no one visible on the burning vessel.

"It looks like a trap!" said the latter. "We had better stand clear of it!"

Even as he spoke, a murmur of alarm arose from the crew of the *Ocean Cloud*, and a steamer was seen moving swiftly towards her.

The waiting spider had detected the presence of its victim.

"It's the *Alabama*," exclaimed Capt. Willis, "and she sees us!"

He put the clipper about and endeavored to escape, but a cannon-ball tore across her deck, very seriously imperiling both Mr. Vale and his daughter, and the piratical cruiser overhauled her so rapidly that the hopelessness of her plight was speedily apparent.

"There's no use of resistance, Edward," said Mr. Vale. "We cannot save the vessel, nor prevent them from taking us prisoners. Any attempts to do so will only anger them. We will surrender!"

The ship was hove to, and the steamer came alongside of her. A boat's crew soon came aboard of the prize, with Capt. Semmes at its head.

"Where's the commander of this ship?" asked the Confederate captain.

Mr. Vale indicated our hero by a gesture.

"Very well, sir. I will trouble you to produce your papers!"

"Never mind the papers!" replied Capt. Willis, who could hardly contain himself under the pirates insolent air. "We sail under the flag of the United States, and hail from Boston!"

Semmes uttered an oath, expressive of his deep satisfaction at this assurance, and then said:

"Such being your character, I have the pleasure of informing you that you are prisoners of war to the Confederate States, steamer *Alabama*, Capt. Semmes!"

Mr. Vale proposed to the captor to bond the vessel, and allow her to proceed on her voyage.

"That business is played out," was the response to this

proposition. "I have adopted the system of destroying every Yankee vessel I encounter. Still, you can show me your documents, and I will decide what to do with you."

Capt. Willis produced the ship's papers, and Semmes ran his eye over them.

"I want a part of your cargo for my own use," he muttered. "All things considered, I think I'll burn the vessel! The fire she'll make may bring another to me!"

"Is this decision irrevocable?"

"Entirely so. I never allow any whining to effect me. And I will now trouble you to attend me to my vessel. Sorry to trouble you, lady, he added, bowing to Ethel, "but such is the fortunes of war. You can take your wardrobe, and any little trinkets that may be in your possession. We always soften these inconveniences all we can to a woman!"

By this time the steamer had laid herself alongside the ship, in obedience to the orders of Capt. Semmes, and a dozen of his followers gathered around him, and were soon engaged in removing the cargo of the *Ocean Cloud* to her captor, with all the noise and rejoicing incidental to such a scene—Capt. Willis, Mr. Vale and Ethel, with the mates and crew of the clipper, were all transferred to the deck of the *Alabama*.

"Your men, captain," said Semmes to our hero, "will have to take their chance in the hold. You two and the lady can remain in my cabin for the present!"

He led the way in that direction, and the trio followed him, Capt. Willis endeavoring to obtain better quarters for his men.

"I hear that the hold of your vessel is a hard place, Capt. Semmes," he finally declared, in plain terms.

"I can't help that," was the reply, uttered in a tone of irritation. "Prisoners of war cannot very well be allowed to be choosers!"

With this Semmes hurried forth to look after the proceedings of his men, leaving the trio in possession of the cabin.

The *Ocean Cloud* was promptly cleared of the best part of her cargo, and then fired, the steamer standing away from her. Semmes waited and watched anxiously, hoping that another prize would be thrown into his hands, but this hope was disappointed.

"Well, better luck next time," he remarked, when the ship had burned to the water's edge. "Perhaps I'll make up for this ill-luck to-morrow!"

He returned to the cabin, showed his prisoners where they could sleep, exchanged a few words with them, and retired to his state-room, locking himself in.

A cry of rejoicing came from the steamer's deck, a few minutes later.

The charred hull of the noble ship, which had so lately been "Walking the waters like a thing of life," had disappeared forever beneath the surface of the ocean.

"Shall we try to sleep, dear father?" asked Ethel, who had watched all these scenes in silent grief. "I do not wish to be separated from you, even for a moment. How terrible all this plundering and burning is! What will they do with us? Is there any danger that they will separate us?"

Before Mr. Vale could reply, Lieut. Murlick, who had been superintending the business of the hour—the removal of the cargo, the securing of the prisoners, and the burning of the ship—came into the cabin.

His eyes met those of Mr. Vale, the two men standing in such a position that the rays of the cabin-lamp fell fully and equally upon them.

They started with mutual exclamations:

"Abner Murlick!"

"Jacob Vale!"

The lieutenant then bent a searching glance upon Ethel, and retreated abruptly to the deck, while the merchant sank into a chair, terribly moved by the unexpected meeting.

"That's your mother's rejected suitor, Ethel!" he whispered to the maiden, as soon as he could command his emotions—"The enemy of whom I was speaking to you this very evening—the man your mother and I suspected of having abducted your lost brother!"

CHAPTER III.

IN CLOSE QUARTERS.

The strangeness of the meeting between Mr. Vale and Murlick—the lapse of time since they had met—the suspicions attaching to the lieutenant respecting the merchants missing boy—the evils the Vale's had to apprehend from their enemy—all these subjects formed the basis of a most exciting discussion between Ethel and her father.

But no light came from this exchange of ideas.

The anxious inquiries rising to the lips of father and daughter remained unanswered.

Had this evil-minded man really abducted Eugene Vale? If so, what had been done with him? Had he grown up in ignorance and in misery? Had the abductor 'maliciously placed him in the lowest walks of life, or turned his young steps into wickedness?

The cold sweat of mental anguish appeared on Mr. Vale's brow, as he considered these questions.

"Not only is this man resting like an incubus on my past, Ethel," he said, "but he gives a dark and menacing aspect to our whole future! What if he should transfer to you the bitter hatred he bore your mother!"

Capt. Willis had heard enough of the conversation to learn that there was some mystery between his friends and the dark-faced lieutenant.

"Don't go, Edward," said Mr. Vale, as the young commander arose with the intention of excusing himself and withdrawing. "We have no privacy from you. I will tell you the whole story!"

He hastened to do so.

"This places us in an awkward position," was our hero's comment. "Still, I think that this man has not influence nor authority enough to harm us. Capt. Semmes has the reputation of being as much of a gentleman as his profession will allow him to be, and we may hope that he will not permit his subordinate to molest us. Moreover, there may be something Providential in your meeting. The mystery respecting the disappearance of your son may be cleared up. If your suspicions are well-founded, the fact will naturally appear in this man's deportment!"

The captives spent some time in conversing upon this subject, and then retired for the night. They slept but little, and were stirring at daylight. At the breakfast-table they met Lieut. Murlick, who glanced at Mr. Vale and our hero, and bestowed a long and searching look upon Ethel, the effect of which was to bring a singular gleam of admiration to his eyes. The repast was nearly concluded, and Capt. Semmes himself had retired from the table, when the villian leaned forward and said to the merchant:

"We were enemies, Mr. Vale, years ago, but the circumstances under which we meet would disarm all bitterness, if I felt any. While you remain here, we can be civil!"

"Just so, sir," replied Mr. Vale, understandingly. "You have my thanks for your consideration!"

The prisoners went on deck after breakfast, and Capt. Willis paid his men a visit, assuring himself that they were as comfortable as they could be in the close and filthy hold into which they had been thrust. They were mostly in irons, and the subordinate officer in charge of them remarked, that, Semmes always treated his prisoners in this manner, to prevent them from rising against him and his crew and seizing the steamer.

The *Alabama* had already renewed her hunt for American vessels, and had a couple of seamen aloft scouring the surface of the ocean with glasses. By the middle of the forenoon a couple of sails were announced, but one of them proved to be a British trader, and the other a Dutch man-of-war. It was not till near nightfall that Semmes encountered

THE OCEAN CLOUD IN FLAMES.

a prize, a New York bark, fresh from Manilla with one-third of a cargo of East Indian productions. As usual, the Confederates fired the vessel soon after dark, and waited for the decoy to bring other victims to them, but none came.

The following day Semmes shaped his course for Mauritius, and kept a strict lookout for prey, but nor a single American ship was encountered. It was natural, perhaps, that he should feel chagrined at this ill-luck.

During these two days Lieutenant Murlick had made a pretence of being busy, and had not uttered any further remarks to Mr. Vale. The suspicious and anxious father had no trouble, however, in observing that the evil eyes of his enemy remained fixed on Ethel every instant she was on deck or otherwise visible.

The third day proved more auspicious to Capt. Semmes, quite a fleet of vessels encountering the steamer. The most of these ships were foreign, or under foreign flags, but three of them were American, two belonging in Boston, and one in New York.

"This looks like doing business," said Semmes to Murlick as they were superintending the preparations for a grand conflagration of the vessels, one after another. "These three ships and their cargoes, with the trifle of specie we've taken, must be worth near a million of dollars!"

Again Semmes lighted up his track with a huge fire, and waited in the background for an additional victim, but he was again disappointed.

"The fact is," he commented, regarding the smouldering and sinking hull of the last vessel, " our fame has preceded us to these waters, and the Yankees are cautious. If they see our fires they steer clear of them!"

In two of these latest captures there had been several lady passengers, enough to fill up every state room in the cabin that was not wanted by the officers of the steamer. Capt. Semmes accordingly concluded, after a conversation with Lieut. Murlick, to send Mr. Vale and Capt. Willis below.

"Perhaps the young lady will object to being separated from her friends," suggested Murlick

"She'll have to do as the rest of the women do," replied Semmes. "It's no place for her down there, that's certain! You'll see to this transfer at once!"

As Murlick turned away, a look singularly expressive of satisfaction appeared on his visage.

"That is a step in the right direction," he muttered. "I wanted to get them separated!"

He entered the cabin, where Mr. Vale was conversing with Ethel and Capt. Willis.

"I am sorry Mr. Vale to be the bearer of bad news to you," he said, bowing politely, and speaking in tones of pretended sympathy," but Capt. Semmes has ordered you to be confined with your men in the hold!"

A general expression of regret followed. Ethel could not restrain her tears.

"What is the cause of this proceeding, Lieutenant Murlick?" asked the merchant.

"It's merely owing to the want of accommodations. Those ladies who fell into our hands this afternoon want all the room there is in the cabin!"

"Then I can go below with my father," said Ethel advancing, and addressing herself directly to Murlick. "I do not wish to be separated from my friends!"

"Sorry, Miss Vale, as I said," rejoined the Lieutenant' again bowing, "but the orders of Captain Semmes are explicit. He cannot allow you in the hold, for it is already packed to overflowing."

"And yet you expect my father and Captain Willis to go there?"

"Oh, they're men, and can do as the rest do, but I assure you that the hold is no place for a woman. You had better take the matter quietly. In a day or two some change for the better will probably be made!"

The trio talked the proposed movement over among themselves, and Mr. Vale finally went on deck, and appealed to Capt. Semmes. The Confederate Commander gruffly replied that he could not revoke the orders that he had given to his executive officer.

"What would you have me do?" he concluded, somewhat petulantly. "You cannot in reason expect me to do better by you. With such a number of prisoners as are now in our hands, we cannot be too guarded. You will have the goodness to go below, sir. As to your daughter, she shall be treated as well as our means will permit—as well as any of the ladies we have taken!"

Mr. Vale returned to his daughter, announcing the result. Ethel gave way to her emotions, expressing her opinion of the captors in plain terms.

"I do not wish to seem harsh," observed Murlick, in the same quiet and hypocritical tones in which he had before spoken, "but I must remind you that other duties are pressing upon me, and that I am waiting to show you the way to the hold!"

He turned away, moving towards the entrance, but took good care to note the particulars of the scene that followed —the tender parting of Ethel from her father and Capt. Willis. The emotion with which she took the hand of the latter, and laid her head on his breast, gave the scheming confederate a very just idea of the feelings existing between the young couple, and brought a deadly gleam to his eyes.

"Be brave, my daughter!" whispered Mr. Vale, embracing her. "These days of trial will soon be over!"

The parting was saddening, and Ethel could not restrain her tears, but—her mind once made up to the hopelessness of attempting resistance or asking for mercy—she comported herself in the most resolute manner. With a tender and affectionate leave-taking, the merchant and the young captain followed Murlick to the hold.

"As I remarked," said the lieutenant, "we are getting well filled up with involuntary passengers. Sorry our accommodations are no better. Can only hope that something will soon occur to your advantage. For the present, in pursuance of the orders of Capt. Semmes, I must chain you to each other and to your fellow prisoners——"

"Chain us?" interrupted Mr. Vale, indignantly.

"Yes, chain you. That is the only way, according to Capt. Semmes, that we can make sure of so many prisoners. I regret this measure as much as you do, but the safety of the vessel seems to require it."

He chained the prisoners closely, and left them, with a hurried adieu. The entrance of the two men had called forth a variety of ejaculations from the young captain's crew, to which he now responped.

The scene of which our hero and Mr. Vale had thus become features—the prison-hold of the *Alabama*—has become as famous in its way, or rather *in*famous, as the Libby prison, at Richmond, so that we may as well briefly describe it.

It was immediately under the main-deck of the steamer, around the main hatch. It had the width of the vessel, and was between thirty-five and forty feet in length. Close, dark and ill-ventilated, under the best of circumstances, it had become doubly disagreeable and unhealthy under the tropical sun, particularly since so many prisoners had been huddled together in it. It contained no berths, no sky-lights, no beds, no blankets.

In this filthy den at the moment Mr. Vale and Capt. Willis were thus introduced into it, were crowded sixty or seventy men of all ages, colors and conditions.

Two or three of them were sick; others were attempting to read by the light of a lantern hanging against the wall; and still others were bemoaning their captivity and complaining of its annoyances and miseries.

The air in this living grave was fetid and feverish, and the prisoners fairly reeked in this close confinement, a hot sweat breaking out on almost every face present.

"An accursed hole, truly!" exclaimed Mr. Vale, as soon as he had realised his surroundings. "How can any person pretending to be civilized thrust a fellow-being into such a place as this?"

He thought of Ethel, with a moan of anguish, and sank down at the feet of Capt. Willis, momentarily unnerved by the horrors of his situation.

"The scene has changed since our boys were brought here," replied our hero. "This overcrowding is horrible!"

Mr. Vale recovered his self-possession.

"Well, let us hope that some good will come to us out of all this evil," he said. "Perhaps these steps are leading us to the discovery of the mystery respecting my lost boy!"

"Heaven grant it!" exclaimed Capt. Willis. "By the way, Mr. Vale, did you see the middy who passed us as we came out of the cabin?"

"No; what middy?"

"A young fellow, about twenty years of age, who bears a singular resemblance to you!"

"To *me?*" responded Mr. Vale, starting to his feet, and becoming deathly pale.

"Yes. The thought occurred to me that he might be your lost son!"

For a moment Mr. Vale was unable to reply. It seemed to him so natural that Murlick should have kept the stolen boy with him (in case he was the abductor,) that the observation of Capt. Willis came upon him with thrilling force.

"I must see to this resemblance," he finally ejaculated. "I feel—I almost know that there is something in it!"

CHAPTER IV.

MURLICK DEVELOPS HIS IDEAS MORE CLEARLY.

The eyes of Lieutenant Murlick flashed wickedly, and his face looked fiendish as he reached the deck after leaving our hero and Mr. Vale in irons.

"That gets them out of my way," he ejaculated. "I shall now have time to tell the fair captive what I think of her."

As he re-entered Ethel's presence, she saw that a change had come over him—that he was now openly cherishing the half-concealed admiration, and vengeful triumph he had experienced during the past three days—that he now deemed himself in a position to reveal his infamous ideas and schemes to her.

"Well, Miss Vale, here we are," was his insulting greeting. "Since the stern fortune of war has taken your natural protector from you, permit me to do what I can to supply his place to you."

His eyes had such a villianous expression that the captive could not endure to look upon him. With a stifled cry of alarm, she turned abruptly away, and locked herself up in the state room that had been assigned to her.

The following morning Ethel wished to pay a visit to her father, and accordingly spoke to Capt. Semmes about it. He referred her to Lieutenant Murlick, as the executive officer of the vessel.

"I don't like to deal with him," she declared.

"You don't? Well I'm sorry for that, but what can I do? Take my advice, young lady, and don't try to choose your company so long as you remain in your present position!"

With this he left her.

For an hour Ethel struggled with her antipathy and half-defined apprehensions, and then she went to Lieutenant Murlick, and informed him that she wished to visit her father.

"Of course, of course!" was his response. "I know your loving heart would soon take you in that direction, and I shall be glad to serve you in the course of half an hour—as soon as my boys have put the decks in order. You can remain in the cabin until I come for you."

The interval thus passed seemed an age, but Murlick finally presented himself before her. She noticed that he had dressed himself with unusual care, and that he was more smiling than she had before seen him.

"I am ready to conduct you to your father, Miss Vale," he said.

Ethel acknowledged the remark with a stately inclination of her head, and followed him to the hold. She was appalled by the odors of the place, and by the spectacle the huddled prisoners presented.

"My father in such a den as this!" she exclaimed, with warm

indignation, as her glances rested on the sea of upturned faces. "What villiany! what baseness!'

"This way, daughter," said her father.

She was shocked by the paleness of his face, as she bounded forward and was clasped to his breast.

"How you have suffered, dear father," she exclaimed, "and all because your kind heart prompted you to come to the supposed relief of others!"

"It is on your account that I have suffered, and not on my own," replied Mr. Vale. "My poor child! What wrong and cruelty oppress you!"

He sobbed in his anguish.

"Oh, for a good breath of air!" he continued, after a pause,—"for room to move about—for a glimpse of the sky or the ocean! It is needless cruelty to shut men up in this manner!"

Ethel fixed upon Murlick such a stern look of rebuke, that he felt called upon to say something apologetical.

"We shall take the hatch off presently, and lower a barrel of water with rations," he said. "There will then be more air."

Ethel now turned to Capt. Willis, who had silently taken her hand, and was waiting for a greeting from her.

"And you, Capt. Willis, how pale you are!" she murmured. "I have been awake all night, thinking of your horrible situation."

"And we have been equally anxious about you!"

The tenderness with which our hero uttered this response caused the maiden to tremble with emotion.

A touching scene followed.

Mr. Vale did not say anything about the mysterious middy, etc., on account of the uncertainty of those subjects.

Lieut. Murlick, as may well be imagined, kept his eyes and ears open, and the manner of the young couple towards each other was sufficiently suggestive to him.

He saw that they were really lovers, whether confessedly so or not, and the knowledge moved him greatly.

His face flushed with a hot gust of passion, and a gleam of infernal meaning appeared in his eyes.

"You must go now, darling," said Mr. Vale, after a brief season of communion with Ethel. "The air is very close here, and I am afraid you will take the fever!"

"God be with you!" said our hero. "Keep up your courage, darling! Be the brave little heart I have ever found you!"

"I will speak to Capt. Semmes, and have you brought on deck, if possible," said the maiden. "I will be hopeful. But you must both be hopeful also!"

A few further expressions of encouragement were exchanged, and Ethel returned to the deck, dismissing Murlick with a bow.

She saw Capt. Semmes and implored him to allow her father and Capt. Willis the freedom of the deck, but her application was fruitless.

"Give one man such a privilege," was the commander's concluding remark, "and all will want it. Your friends shall not long remain in confinement. I shall send them ashore as soon as I get over-crowded!"

This assurance was the first consoling word she had had from him. She thanked him, and returned to the cabin.

Capt. Semmes continued his hunt during the day. He boarded several vessels, and captured one—a ship belonging in Philadelphia. At night, he had his conflagration, as usual, but gained no additional victim by it.

This day was a continual pang to Ethel, as to her father and Capt. Willis. She remained constantly in the cabin, affording such consolation to the other lady prisoners as her superior intellect and firmness enabled her to impart to them. She encountered Murlick at meals and every time she went on deck, and his eyes followed her movements, but he did not actually insult her. After another long night of anguish and restlessness, she resolved again to see her father and Capt. Willis.

"Is there no way of obtaining their enlargement of

Capt. Semmes?" she inquired of Murlick, after stating her wishes.

"May be," he replied, with his eyes resting upon the maiden's lovely face in a stare of wrapt admiration. "Capt. Semmes might say yes, if I were to champion their cause."

"Will you speak a word for them?"

"That depends on yourself!" he pointedly replied.

"On me? How?"

"Why, if you treat me in a friendly manner, I will reciprocate. It cannot be unknown to you that I am the executive officer of this vessel. Neither can it be unknown to you that I can give your friends the liberty of the deck, if I choose to do so!"

This was putting the case plainly. Ethel opened her eyes, both literally and figuratively.

"Well, why have you not done so," she demanded. "You have seen my anguish—you know how they suffered!"

Murlick smiled grimly.

"Really, you have not put yourself in communication with me," he said. "How can we do favors for people who disdain to speak to us? True, I might have proceeded to serve you, on my own authority, under the assumption that such and such a course would be agreeable to you—but, really, that is not the regular way of getting at such matters. In a word, if you want my good offices, you can at least ask me civilly for them!"

He chuckled to himself wickedly, by way of conclusion. He felt that he had spoken sagaciously—that he had, in fact, deftly paved the way for a more intimate acquaintance with the captive.

"To tell the truth, Lieut. Murlick," replied Ethel, "I did not suppose it would do any good to ask your assistance."

"In other words, your father has painted me as a fiend, and so caused you to treat me as one? I regret your mistake."

The scheming villian had now made his authority sufficiently plain to Ethel for her to be desirous of conciliating him. How should she proceed?

"My father told me of the difficulty between you and my mother, years ago," she said, "and I naturally felt an aversion towards you, under the circumstances of our meeting. We suspected you, moreover, of having been instrumental in the disappearance of my only brother, in his infancy——"

"You suspected me?" interrupted Murlick, starting.

"Certainly." she boldly replied. "Why not? You uttered threats—many of them—which have had no fulfillment, unless in that sad affliction!"

Murlick paced back and forth a few times, regarding the maiden attentively, and then said:

"True, I did utter some threats against your parents, at the period referred to, but they were forgotten as soon as uttered. I loved your mother, and was half-maddened by her preference of your father, but such emotions do not last. A tender respect for your mother's memory is the only sentiment with which I recall all those matters!"

"And you had nothing to do with the abducting of my brother?"

"Nothing. I was in business in New Orleans, and did not even know that your parents had any children. I have not heard of them since the summer after their marriage!"

Ethel marked the sinister expression of his face, and felt that he was lying, but she did not care to say so. She merely remarked:

"This is a very gratifying assurance!"

"Let it be the basis of our friendship," replied Murlick, advancing towards her. "I loved your mother, and had the greatest admiration for her. Pardon me for adding, that the little I have seen of you has awakened similar emotions. The affection I bore your mother is transferred to you."

The tone in which he spoke, his mien, and the expression of his face, all startled Ethel. She retreated from him, suppressing a cry of surprise.

What do you mean?" she said. "Your words—your whole conduct is insulting!"

"Oh, no; do not say so!" he said, with eyes glowing like live coals. "I speak as a friend—as one who loves you."

"Sir, no more of this—not another word, or I will report your conduct to Capt. Semmes! Surely he will not permit his officers to insult his prisoners!"

At this instant Capt. Semmes came out of the cabin. Ethel was aroused, not only in resentment of Murlick's conduct, but also under the conviction that he had been (notwithstanding his denial) concerned in the abduction of her brother. She accordingly turned to the Confederate commander, and commenced talking confidentially with him.

The manner in which Murlick met this crisis was worthy of him. He waited quietly, with a glance of assumed pity on his face until Semmes looked at him, with a glance that meant, "What is that she's saying?" and then he tapped his forehead significantly, and turned aside, and scanned the surface of the water. Semmes soon shook off the maiden, and rejoined his subordinate, while she hurried to the cabin.

"What is the matter with this young lady, Lieut. Murlick?" was the Captain's inquiry.

"Can't say, Captain," was the reply. I suspect, however, that the anxiety and strangeness of her lot has touched her in the upper story. Why, she says that you have stolen her brother!"

"The deuce she does!" exclaimed Semmes. "Ha, ha! she told me that *you* stole him!"

"The two men laughed uproriously.

"A good joke," added Semmes. "She says that her mother's in love with you, and that terrible threats were uttered by you, and all that. Keep your eye on her, Murlick, and see that she does no injury to herself or any one else. "After all," he added, becoming serious "it's a sad case."

He passed on to attend to some duty. Murlick looked after him, with a strangely jubilant manner.

"That's another good move!" he muttered. "He thinks

she's insane, and will say she's gone overboard, should she be suddenly missing. Ha, ha!"

As he went about his duties, it was remarked, that he was singularly excited. And he chuckled frequently to himself like one already sure of the success of some awful scheme.

The *Alabama* passed another unsuccessful day steaming steadily towards Maritius. The fright Murlick had given Ethel caused her to remain secluded in her stateroom, and to have her dinner and supper brought to her by a fellow captive. Her desolation and anguish may be imagined.

The next day was more fortunate for the Confederates.

Soon after daylight, a large ship was seen standing to the eastward, on the extreme horizon, and a lively and exciting chase ensued resulting in the capture of the stranger, which proved to belong in Boston. She had a valuable cargo, a large crew, and ten or twelve passengers, including several women and children. Placed in charge of a prize crew, she followed in the wake of the Confederate steamer during the day, very readily keeping up with her. The accession of prisoners gained from this vessel filled the hold of the *Alabama* to overflowing, and caused Semmes to resolve on sending them all ashore the following day, in accordance with his usual custom.

"We had better land them at the Cape," he said to Murlick, after the latter had reported to him that a couple of the prisoners had died in the hold, either of disease or suffocation. "We shall have to use one of our prizes for this purpose, of course. Shall we take this clipper?"

Murlick was determined to prolong his association with Miss Vale just as long as he could, and he accordingly replied:

"I would not send them ashore now, nor until you get a poorer vessel. Suppose this one should be recaptured by the *Vanderbilt* or some other federal cruiser, on approaching the Cape? She's too valuable to the Yankees for us to run any risk of restoring her to them. We'd better burn her to-night, and take the chances of getting another for the use of the prisoners!"

This sinister advice was adopted.

The track of Semmes to the eastward was again lighted up, immediately after night-fall, by the wanton destruction of his prize.

Contrary to the expectation of Murlick, the light of the conflagration brought a victim to the scene—a handsome clipper-bark hailing from New York.

"This is just the craft for the landing of the prisoners," observed Semmes to his lieutenant, when the bark was fully in his possession. "We'll start her for the shore forthwith, and you shall have charge of the whole matter. After landing the prisoners at the Cape, or at Cape Town, just as you choose—you can report to me at our retreat at the Dodo Islands!"

Murlick was placed quite at his ease by learning that he was to have charge of the prisoners.

"Shall I start to-night?" he asked.

"Yes, as soon as we can transfer the prisoners to the prize. See to it, that they are securely ironed!"

The joy of Murlick was great, as he superintended the removal of the prisoners from the steamer to the bark. He saw that he would have the Vales completely at his mercy. The male prisoners were all put in the hold of the prize, and chained hand and foot, while the ladies and children were assigned places in the cabin. The hull of the last decoy had scarcely disappeared beneath the waves, when Murlick reported to his superior officer that he was ready for departure.

"Well, I believe everything is understood between us," responded Semmes. "I shall proceed to the Dodos in the morning, and probably do but little more business until you return to us. I wish to put a new coat of paint on the steamer, and otherwise disguise her. Take care of yourself and good-luck to you!"

Murlick uttered his orders to his brother officers, and went aboard of the bark. The crew detailed to her from the *Alabama* went about their duties, with a hearty cheer, and she stood away before the wind for Cape Town. In a few minutes she was beyond sight or hearing from the steamer, and Murlick's lawless sense of freedom was complete.

Everything had gone to his liking!

Leaning over the bulwarks near him was Ethel Vale, pale and excited, in momentary expectation of some further display of his brutality. Below, in the darkness of the hold, lay her father and Capt. Willis, writhing in chains, and overwhelmed with the most terrible anxiety and foreboding. And around the scheming lieutenant were twelve or fifteen of his fellow-ruffians, all ready for the execution of his will.

It was no wonder that he smiled! No wonder that his eyes gleamed savagely, as he whispered to himself:

"She is even more beautiful than her mother, and I love her already far better than I loved her mother before her! Lovely and enchanting creature! she shall speedily be mine!"

CHAPTER V.

A MOVE IN THE RIGHT DIRECTION.

WE must now see how Capt. Willis and Mr. Vale were getting along in their close quarters.

After the visit of Ethel to them, accompanied by Murlick, they had experienced a conviction that the villian meant her and them a positive evil.

They had sent for Capt. Semmes, with the intention of mentioning this apprehension, but he had been, thus far, too busy to come near them.

They had endeavored to learn something about the midshipmen who resembled the merchant, but in vain.

They had sent for Ethel repeatedly, but their messages had not been taken to her.

The horrible anxieties which had thus grown upon them, can be imagined.

After the transfer of the prisoners to the bark, it was no longer possible for the father and lover to doubt that Murlick meant them ill.

The scheming miscreant had assured himself, with his own eyes, that their irons were sound; and had taken care that they should not see the maiden during the process of their removal from one vessel to the other.

The only deduction they could make from his conduct was that he was maturing some infamous scheme against Ethel and themselves.

They were accordingly discussing the probable character of his villiany, at the instant he was expressing his vengeful glee, as recorded.

How will the blow come, Ned?" asked Mr. Vale. "Will he land us, and retain Ethel in his custody? Will he threathen to set us ashore on some desolate island, if she does not consent to marry him? My God! what is the form in which his baseness and malignancy will find expression?"

"It is hard to say," replied our hero, in a voice that quivered with his intense grief and anxiety. "The only certainty, is that he means us evil! He will not land us at the Cape, with the other prisoners—or, if he does, he will bear Ethel away with him. Now that he is out of Semmes sight, he we will pause at nothing that feeds his revenge!"

Mr. Vale could only groan, by way of reply.

Capt. Willis was silent a moment, surveying the scene around him—the prisoners, the guard at the entrance, and the various objects in the hold, all revealed by the dim light of a lantern hanging against the wall. He then placed his lips to Mr. Vale's ear, and whispered:

"We cannot act too soon!"

"True—but I see no chance for action, What can we do? What would you say?"

"We must strike for our freedom!"

The merchant started at this brief communication, and stared fixedly at the speaker.

"What is it Ned?" he soon demanded. "Give me your idea—for I see that you have one!"

"Yes. Speak low and I will tell you my meaning. I discovered soon after we were put into the hold of the steamer, that I could *slip my handcuffs!*"

Mr. Vale was speechless with a joyful surprise.

"You know I am of slender build," pursued our hero, "and have a small hand. While we were on the steamer, surrounded by her whole crew, I did not care to mention the fact, lest I should arouse vain hopes, but there's no mistake about it!"

"Well, what do you propose to do?"

"To make a move in the right direction. We have had enough of this sort of things—enough of chains and separation! I may fail—but I'd rather be at the bottom of the sea, than where I am at this moment!"

"I share the feeling, Ned. Poor Ethel! But how will you strike?"

"Leave all to me. I'll take the first step now."

He produced a piece of fat pork he had saved from the soup furnished him, and greased his hands with it, rubbing them till they were moist. He then applied himself to the self-prescribed task—that of slipping his handcuffs. The bones of his hands fairly cracked under the pressure of the encircling steel, but he persisted in the measure, and in a moment the long-fettered member was free.

"That's the main thing," he whispered. "The rest is easy!"

"Heaven grant it, Ned. Everything now depends upon you!"

Ned was silent a moment, as if rallying all his forces for the coming struggle, and then whispered:

"There are over a hundred of us. Two-thirds of this number will fight to the death, if I can furnish them arms. There are only twelve or fifteen of the pirates. This guard has the keys of our irons—or did, when we were on the steamer. He will transfer them to the men who relieves him, and it's about time for that man to appear. When he comes——"

The party referred to was already heard coming.

He proved to be a burly confederate, who approached snapping and snarling, and wishing that the prisoners had been at the bottom of the sea before he was detained to watch them. He relieved his predecessor, and received from him the keys mentioned, with a few words of instruction.

"The critical moment has come!" whispered Ned, as the relieved man withdrew. "This fresh guard will be along in a moment, to see if we are safe!"

Mr. Vale fairly held his breath.

Two or three of his fellow prisoners detected that some project was on foot, and were watching intently for its denoument.

The guard took the lantern from the wall, and commenced a tour of inspection through the hold, in accordance with his instructions.

Ned had secured, and brought with him from the steamer a pair of heavy shackles which had been taken from one of the prisoners who had died there, and he now held them doubled in his hand, ready for their intended work.

As the guard came within reach of him, and was inspecting the shackles of Mr. Vale, Ned struck him a terrific blow and he fell senseless to the floor.

A buzz of excitement arose from the prisoners who had been watching the proceedings, and some of their sleeping comrades started out of their slumber, with ejaculations of inquiry and alarm.

"Silence, every man of you!" commanded Ned. "Silence! and I will release you!"

The injunction was obeyed.

The lantern had been overthrown in the fall of the guard, but was not extinguished, and Mr. Vale instantly picked it up, whispering:

"Now for the keys!"

Ned searched the pockets of the prostrate man, and produced the keys. In a moment, while the merchant held the light, our hero released Mr. Vale and himself.

"Me next!" exclaimed half a score of voices, in chorus. "Here! here!"

"Patience, men," responded Ned, with a calm cheerfulness that allayed the rising panic. "I will attend to you as fast as I can. The first measure is to obtain arms!"

He seized the cap and coat of the insensible guard, as well as his weapons, and then added:

"Take the light and the keys, Mr. Vale, and release all the men you can in my absence. I am going to look for sabres and pistols. We can do nothing without them!"

The prisoners felt the necessity of this measure, and each resigned himself to it.

"Silence, all!" was Ned's parting injunction. "A breath, and we are lost!"

He hurried to the entrance, and in another moment gained the deck.

He halted in the shadow of the sails, and looked around him.

The night was serenely beautiful.

A flood of mellow moonlight lighted up the scene, and the starry hosts were revealed in the clear splendor of the tropics.

Scattered along the deck of the vessel was the watch on duty, each individual engaged at some task, or conversing with his fellows, so that the appearance of our hero in their midst was not particularly noticed.

With what a thrill of joy he exulted in his regained freedom.

How tenderly and wildly he thought of Ethel.

Where was Murlick? Where could he find some arms? How best avoid detection?

He took off his boots, and stole toward the cabin.

Listening at the head of the companion way, and hearing

nothing to alarm him, he crept down the stairs, pausing at their foot, and looking searchingly around.

A dim light was burning in a swinging lantern in the centre of the cabin, and by its rays Ned beheld a couple of women in one of the rear state-rooms.

As the nearest of these ladies changed her position, he beheld Ethel seated at a little table, her head leaning on her hand, and her attitude one of despair.

One of her companions addressed her, and as she roused up to reply, she disclosed a face of such pallor and sadness that Capt. Willis yearned over her with a great flood of pity and tenderness.

He saw that the ladies were bidding the maiden good-night, and retreated to the head of the stairs, not caring to run the risk of such an alarm as they were likely to raise at the detection of his presence. They soon left her, however, shutting themselves up in an adjoining state-room, and Ned then moved cautiously towards her. His movements, as stealthy as they were, were detected by her acute hearing, and she looked up. As she knew how strongly the prisoners were chained, and how closely they were guarded, the first thought that presented itself to her mind was that she saw an apparition, and a wild look of terror appeared on her face.

"Hush, darling! Do not speak—do not be afraid of me! It is me!"

He took her by the hand.

"O, God!" she murmured. "Can I believe my sight—my hearing?"

An instant longer she looked admiringly at him, as she instinctively closed the door of the state-room, and then she threw herself into his arms. She nestled in his bosom. She rained kisses upon his cheeks and lips. She clung to his neck, weeping for joy. She panted in her half-delirious excitement.

"My father?" she finally murmured.

"Is free also, and engaged in releasing our fellow-prisoners," replied our hero. "We are going to strike for our freedom. Where's Murlick?"

"In a state-room on the opposite side of the cabin. He has been there but few a minutes. Can it be that he is already asleep?"

They both listened, Ethel partly disengaging herself from Ned's embrace, and blushing at her late impulsiveness. She was the first to speak.

"I'll see what he's about," she whispered. "Please remain where you are!"

She slipped out of the state-room, closing the door behind her. She returned, after the lapse of a minute or two, and whispered:

"I hear nothing of him. He may be asleep, and may be looking over the papers of the late captain of this vessel. It will be safe for us to be on our guard against the villain. Why did not father come with you?"

Ned briefly explained, adding:

"You see that we want arms. Can you assist us to find some?"

"Yes, Murlick stowed quite a lot of them away in the state room next to this. Perhaps my key will fit the door. Let's see!"

She tried it. The door opened.

"Step in!" she said. "I will listen again."

Ned stepped into the state-room, and found a dozen swords and as many pistols, mostly revolvers. He tied them all in two bunches, running a noose tie through the handles of the former, and a stout cord he happened to have through the handles of the latter.

"The way is clear," whispered Ethel, returning to him. "I hear nothing of Murlick. He thinks the game is all in his own hands, and is resting from his late watchfulness on the *Alabama*."

"May he awake in our hands!" responded Ned, as he came out of the state-room. "Be brave now, Ethel. You soon shall see your father. These arms are our salvation!"

These words, in connection with the bright and cheery

look on the speakers countenance, inspired Ethel with hope and faith.

"Heaven be with you!" she rejoined. "I shall be in my apartment. Tell father to be cautious for my sake, and to hurry to me as soon as he can!"

At this juncture, just as Ned was going, Murlick appeared in the door-way of his state-room, looking from one to the other.

CHAPTER VI.

MURLICK BIDES HIS TIME.

The meeting was a mutual one, but Murlick, having supposed his prisoners secure, was considerably the most startled, and stood motionless a moment, like one paralyzed.

That momentary inaction cut him dearly.

Without a word or any display of his emotions, Ned leaped at his enemy, taking him by the throat, with the intention of preventing him from summoning assistance.

The struggle that followed can be imagined—the panting of the combatants; their fierce grapple, as they rolled over and over! the scuffling of feet; the beating of heads and limbs against the walls of the state-room; the awful ferocity of Murlick, contrasted with the quiet resolution of our hero; and the anxiety with which Ethel watched them.

It was a desperate and prolonged battle.

The ladies opened their state-room doors and looked out, some with faint screams, some in a horrified silence. And it was thus that Ethel evinced the stuff of which she was made, she moving from one to the other of the frightened ones, enjoining them to be still, assuring them that all was well and would soon be better!

She had seen that Ned, having closed his fingers on Murlick's throat, had the advantage from the start, and that he had maintained it. Gasping and discolored, Murlick ceased his struggle, and the victor, with the aid of Ethel, gagged and bound him, and locked him up in the state-room.

"That's good for us!" said Ned, after looking out from the cabin. "No alarm has been raised, and we can now go on with our proceedings!"

He picked up his swords and pistols, addressed a few further words to Ethel, enjoining her to keep the women quiet, and then hurried from the cabin.

The posture of affairs on deck was very much as he had left it.

One of the sailors on duty was engaged in spinning an interesting yarn, and several of his comrades had neither eyes nor ears for anything else.

In a moment Ned had gained the hold, with his weapons, and his triumphant return was hailed by the prisoners with a wild buzz of excitement.

He found that more than thirty of them had been restored to the use of their limbs, and that the rest were being attended to with all possible expedition.

"Be cautious, men!" said Capt. Willis, in a low but perfectly distinct tone. "Our lives still depend upon your caution!"

There was instant silence, while he distributed the swords and pistols as far as they would go, arming Mr. Vale with the rest.

"I secured all the arms that were not in use," he then said. "I will now go to the forecastle, where the watch off duty is sleeping, and secure their weapons!"

"Oh, no, Ned!" exclaimed Mr. Vale, grasping the young captain's hand. "I can't consent to your taking such a risk. We have weapons for more than a dozen of us, and there are not more than fifteen of our enemies on board. We can conquer them. You must not go!"

"Their fifteen pistols would kill fifteen of us," responded Ned, quietly. "We must have their arms, not only for our own use, but to deprive them of them! Let what will occur, I can make my way back to you, or give you notice of trouble. I must go!"

Mr. Vale pressed his hand with deep emotion, and Capt. Willis added:

"Ethel is all safe in the cabin, and longing to see you! Have faith and patience!"

He again slipped upon deck, and gained the forecastle unsuspected, but not unnoticed. Its occupants, the watch off duty, were asleep. A lantern was burning dimly, revealing the sleepers in their bunks, and some weapons scattered about on the tables and stools, and as many more hung over their sleeping owners. As Ned entered, one or two of the seamen turned over, muttering incoherently. As silently as possible, the intruder began to collect the scattered arms, securing them as he had done those in the state-room, and he soon possessed all that were visible.

He now breathed more freely.

He was resolved, however, not to leave a single weapon to imperil the lives of his friends, if he could help it, and he began feeling under the heads of the sleepers.

"What do you want here?" growled one of the seamen, impatiently, as he half-roused himself from his slumber at Ned's touch.

"I want your weapon!" said Capt. Willis, in a low and steady tone. "Ah! here it is!"

After a few further successes, Ned concluded that he had obtained nearly all of the arms on board of the vessel, except such as might be in possession of the watch on deck, and prepared to return to his companions.

He left the forecastle, with a watchful eye and no little anxiety, but with a jubilant thrill pervading his whole being. While passing along the deck, he was seen by one of the men on duty, and suddenly seized, while the fellow uttered a wondering exclamation.

Capt. Willis instantly realized not only his own peril, but the danger his friends would be in should the arms in his possession be recaptured.

A quick glance showed him that the other sailors on deck were not noticing himself nor the confederate detaining him.

With the quickness of a flash, and while the fellow was tightening his grip, and in the act of uttering an outcry, Capt. Willis struck him with his revolver, and he fell to the deck with a dull sound.

The noise aroused his companions, and they rushed forward, uttering cries of alarm, as Ned dashed into the hold, exclaiming :

"Lively, men! Take these arms. The pirates have detected me, but are almost without weapons. We are four to one. Let the unarmed remain here to release the rest of you, while we gain possession of the vessel. Everything is in our own hands. Come, men. Follow me!"

He led the way to the deck, and the men poured after him. Their appearance was greeted by the confederates with a general shout of consternation. To Ned's surprise, Murlick was on the deck, near the forecastle, at the head of his followers, two or three of them having dashed into the cabin and released him.

"Now, men, for our freedom!" cried Capt. Willis, in a voice like the roar of a lion. "Forward, all together!"

As completely as he had been taken by surprise by the movement of our hero, Murlick was neither subdued nor daunted. To his original hatred of the Vales, he had added a bitter feeling of jealousy of Capt. Willis, and a still fiercer sentiment of love for Ethel, and all these passions and emotions combined made him a most formidable foe to encounter.

"Turn out, boys!" he shouted, with a glance towards the forecastle. "Secesh against the Yankees forever!"

As bravely as he spoke, he speedily saw enough to cause him to quail—the watch off duty pouring unarmed out of the forecastle, and the late prisoners gathering in overwhelming array before him.

He saw that an hour of retribution had come.

Maddened with desperation, he attacked our hero furiously, and a sharp conflict succeeded.

His followers made a desperate onslaught upon their late

prisoners, but he and they speedily saw that the odds against them were fatal.

Capt. Willis had fairly beaten Murlick, when he caught sight of Mr. Vale struggling in the grasp of a frenzied assailant, and sprang to his rescue, cutting the fellow down at his feet. At the same instant, one of the Confederates, beside himself with fright, leaped on the bulwarks and plunged overboard. Another exclaimed that he surrendered, and the cry became a chorus, so that the victors stayed their hands.

A bubbling shriek came up from the water, and a large portion of the federals hurried to the other side of the bark and looked after the drowning man as he fell astern in the darkness, although he was out of sight. Some spoke of heaving to and lowering a boat, and others said it would be of no avail to do so. Our hero was busy with Mr. Vale. And in this general confusion, Murlick found himself detached from the group, near the forecastle, unnoticed, and so thoroughly vanquished that no one cared for his whereabouts.

"If I can hide unseen," he thought, "and remain undetected, they'll think that it was I that jumped overboard!"

His legs moved even more rapidly than his thoughts, and he was speedily in the forecastle.

Much to his joy he found a passage leading into the lower hold. He was soon far down among the boxes and bales stowed in that part of the vessel, groping his way in utter darkness.

He had recently broken cargoes enough to know where everything was kept, and he made his way to the water-casks, tappping them until he found one that was empty.

By a herculean exertion of his strength, he moved some of the full casks sufficiently to admit of his placing the empty one among them.

With the aid of an oaken lever that came opportunely to his hands—it being habitually used to move the casks—he dashed in the head of the empty one, which he then inserted over his shoulders. Crouching, the cask touched the floor, and he was completely shut in.

Placing his mouth near the bung-hole, he settled himself into an easy posture, and listened.

"They may find me here," he muttered, "and they may not. If they don't, I'll bide my time!"

He chuckled to himself and, with the air of one who considers himself dangerous and unconquered, and continued to listen.

CHAPTER VII.

THE RETURN TO THE CAPE.

The victory was won, and Capt. Willis and his friends remained in possession of the vessel.

It was speedily ascertained that two of the Confederates were killed and one badly wounded, while, with the exception of a few slight wounds, the victors were uninjured.

Ned's crew surrounded him, with noisy acclamations and shouts of rejoicing.

His attention being called to the fact that a man was overboard, the young captain hove to, and ordered out a boat to look for him. The cries of the drowning man had now died away, however, and the boat came back unsuccessful, and the bark resumed her course.

Our hero noticed that the man at the wheel was intelligent looking, and that he was apparently unmoved by the scene around him. He questioned him in regard to his strange behaviour, and asked him why he had not assisted his fellow-seamen.

"Because," replied the man, still attending to his duty, "my business is here, and I did not want anything to do with the fighting?"

A general laugh followed this remark, and he added:

"To tell the truth, I can imagine worse misfortunes than

to be under the old flag, or a prisoner in the hands of its defenders!"

Ned instantly comprehended that the man was more than half Unionist, and he replied:

"You can retain your freedom, and consider yourself our guest, not a prisoner!"

The captain of the bark having been killed at the time of her capture by the *Alabama*, it was unanimously agreed that Capt. Willis should take command of her, and he immediately ordered a man to the wheel, relieving the Confederate, and selected a watch from his men for the remainder of the night.

Two-thirds of the Confederates had gathered in a group about their dead and wounded comrades, and, throwing down their arms, had repeated their surrender. Some of them were sullen, and defiant, and others appeared overwhelmed with fear. The remainder of their number were hunted out of the cabin, forecastle, and lower hold, and brought to the deck. Although the hunters passed near Murlick in his concealment, they did not detect his presence, and returned to Ned with the conclusion that the villain was the man who had plunged overboard.

The dead Confederates were sewed up in sail-cloth and launched into the sea, with brief ceremonies, and the wounded one was removed to the forecastle and humanely cared for.

The remaining prisoners were ironed and put in the hold, the universal voice of the captors being in favor of this treatment.

"We will not treat them as badly as we have been treated," said Capt. Willis, "but we will nevertheless let them know what it is to be prisoners!"

The confederates being thus disposed of, a guard was put over them, and the captors made themselves comfortable. The passengers of the different vessels were assigned places in the cabin, as far as it would contain them, and some spare sails were speedily converted into an awning to shelter the rest. The sailors took possession of the forecastle, and as much of the forward deck as they required.

When everything was arranged to his liking, Ned proceeded to Ethel's state-room, where she and her father were still engaged in conversation, and was instantly admitted. He was welcomed by Ethel with a warm pressure of the hand, and a vivid blush, while Mr. Vale exclaimed:

"Ethel has been telling me, Ned, of your fight with Murlick. You're a brave and noble fellow—I wish you were my son!"

Ethel's blushes deepened, and Ned quickly replied:

"You can make me so, sir! Will you give me Ethel?"

The merchant looked from one to the other of the young couple and then said:

"I don't know of any man on earth, my dear boy, to whom I would so willingly entrust the future of my child as to you! You can have her, with her father's blessing, if she's willing!"

Ned whispered to the maiden, and that her answer was satisfactory, was plainly evinced by the light that suddenly overspread the young captain's countenance, and the betrothal kiss he bestowed upon her.

Mr. Vale was fairly overcome with delight.

He had long known the sterling qualities of Ned's head and heart, and regarded him already as a dear son.

"And now," said Ned, a few minutes later, when they had rejoiced with each other sufficiently, "we are having a grand supper in the cabin! Let us take our place among the rest!"

They went into the large apartment, and found the table already spread, and the late prisoners grouped around the apartment partaking of a supper.

"And so we are all very comfortable," said Ned to Ethel, when he had supplied her plate and his own, and had found seats. "What joy it is for me to be again with you—under such circumstances too!"

Ethel encountered his ardent and loving gaze, and, to conceal the emotion that was plainly shown in her scarlet cheeks and sparkling eyes, she said :

"Do you believe that Murlick is really dead? Perhaps he is hidden somewhere in the vessel. I have not yet dismissed all my fears of him!"

"That's because you have been so completely terrified by him!" replied Ned. "This feeling will wear off. His own men say he's jumped overboard, and that's the very course such a villain would take in his desperation, he being too fierce and defiant to surrender. We'll search the vessel thoroughly, however," he added, "and so make sure of being rid of him!"

As soon, therefore, as they had finished their repast, Capt. Willis, aided by Mr. Vale and half a score of the passengers, searched the ship thoroughly, passing near the place of Murlick's concealment and even sounding some of the water-casks around him, thereby causing the villain's heart to quake with fear. Not finding any trace of him, the conviction became general that the man who had jumped overboard was really Murlick.

Capt. Willis decided to keep on his course to the Cape, in order to land the Confederates and such of the federals as might wish to take passage thence in homeward bound vessels. It was his intention to retain command of the bark, ample provisioning her at Cape Town, and take her to New York, carrying with him as many of the passengers as he could, and there have the Courts pass upon his claim to her.

The succeeding days passed pleasant, and the occupants of the bark spent much of their time on deck, telling stories, playing games, and otherwise exercising and enjoying their new-found freedom. Nothwithstanding the faithful performance of his duties as captain, Ned found time to devote himself to Ethel and to make the days pass like a blissful dream to her.

Except their manacles and shackles, the prisoners in the hold, were well-cared for, allowed plenty of fresh air and good food, and otherwise kindly treated.

About sunset, on the third day after taking the vessel

Capt. Willis sailed into Table Bay. The passengers thronged the deck, and witnessed with delight the halo of crimson and amber clouds that crowned the bow of Table Mountain, the palms and other trees that lined the shores, and finally the castle, the fortress and batteries that guarded the harbor and town.

The village with its regular streets and neat brick houses, its government buildings, etc., presented a home-look to the tired passengers, and they requested to go ashore immediately—some wishing to procure clothes, others to mail letters, and others to "get a good sleep," as one of the ladies declared.

The surf of the Atlantic against the shores at Cape Town,, sometimes rendering anchoring impracticable, and it was sometime before a safe anchorage was effected. The boats were then got out and the passengers and crews were taken ashore, load after load, until the bark was nearly deserted, Capt. Willis then changed the guard over his prisoners, and said to Ethel and her father, who stood leaning over the bulwarks and contemplating the scene:

"I must go ashore to procure provisions for our journey across the Atlantic. There remain goods enough on board to exchange for all we want, and we can obtain some money, if necessary. Would'nt you like to go to the town, Ethel, with me, and purchase something for your wardrobe?"

"I think not to-day, Edward, was the reply. "Father has a headache, and I will stay with him. Besides, you know I have my trunks all safe. But we'll all go in the morning!"

Capt. Willis kissed his betrothed and then climbed down into his boat and was rowed ashore, Ethel and her father watching him until he landed.

In this posture of affairs, a sinister event occurred.

Lieut Murlick peered out of the forecastle, surveying the deck, the father and daughter, the town, and the whole scene around him!

CHAPTER VIII.

ANOTHER SUDDEN CHANGE OF FORTUNE.

The face of the Confederate lieutenant was haggard, almost wild in its expression. His fare, since the night of the conflict, had consisted of sea biscuits and water, and his sleep had not extended beyond a few snatches of dozing. He had early realized that the bark was making for the Cape, as fast as the wind could carry her, and had grimly awaited events. He had not shown himself to his men, although he had made a stealthy visit to that quarter of the vessel, and informed himself of their situation.

His appearance, as he thus looked forth upon Mr. Vale and Ethel, was startling—his features glowing with his emotions, and his eyes gleaming like those of a hungry beast of prey. In his hand he held the heavy lever with which he had knocked in the head of the hogshead which for three days and nights had been his retreat.

"I see! The field is ready for the sower!" was his half-audible comment on the situation of affairs. "I will hasten to improve it!"

He hastened to the hold, lever in hand. One of Ned's men was keeping guard over the prisoners, but in an indolent and careless way, having no apprehensions of a rescue. He was seated on a low stool, with his back to the wall, and engaged in smoking. With a chuckle of delight, Murlick levelled him with a single blow of his weapon, and then said:

"Not a word, men—not a whisper! I am here, and I bring you your freedom!"

He took the keys from the pocket of the insensible guard, and restored his men to liberty one after another.

As the men arose and stretched their limbs, they expressed their joy.

"This way, men," said Murlick. "I will furnish you arms. There are enough of them in the forecastle. The Yankees have nearly all gone ashore, and we shall have no difficulty in recapturing the vessel!"

The assurance excited his men so much that he could hardly restrain them. Expressions of vindictiveness burst from them, as they followed their leader to the forecastle.

"You shall have full satisfaction for your confinement," said Murlick, as he saw that this part of the vessel was entirely deserted. "Here are plenty of swords and pistols, the very same taken from us by the Yankees. Help yourselves to them!"

The men selected their arms, while Murlick peered forth upon the deck, which still remained as quiet as at the moment of his previous survey. The father and daughter still remained leaning over the bulwarks, and were conversing in low tones with each other, all unsuspicious of the startling events which had just taken place behind them. The realization of their unprotectedness filled the soul of the observer with an infernal delight.

He crept back to his fellows, giving expression to his emotions in a low chuckle.

"Prepare for action, men," he commanded. "You will not shoot any one except in case of actual necessity. Await orders and keep cool!"

He went up to the deck followed by his men, and approached the father and daughter.

As they drew near, Mr. Vale looked up. An expression of consternation and terror appeared on his face as he recognized his enemy, and he hurriedly drew his pistol, while Ethel uttered a low cry of alarm.

"Don't you use that weapon!" said Murlick, in an ugly tone, "or I'll have you shot on the spot! I am master of this vessel. I have watched my chance and I know that nearly everybody has gone ashore, and I am quite competent to take care of those that remain. Will you surrender?"

Mr. Vale could not reply. All things seemed to reel before him at this new misfortune. Ethel was dumb with grief.

"You may as well," pursued Murlick. "Capt. Willis won't be back just at present. No resistance can avail!"

The merchant moaned in his terrible anguish. Ethel recovered her calmness and spoke for him.

"Since resistance is useless, as you say, we will surrender," she said. "You will permit us to retire to my state-room?"

"Yes, but I will first clear the cabin," replied Murlick. "You can remain here in charge of men my till I return."

He selected several of his men and immediately seized every man on the bark, with the exception of Mr. Vale, and shut them up in the hold. He then visited the cabin, locking up the women he found therein in a couple of state-rooms. He then returned to Mr. Vale and Ethel.

"You will not dare perpetrate this seizure in neutral waters, Lieut. Murlick," said the merchant. "My daughter and I are now under the protection of the English government!"

"Oh you are?" was the insulting response. "Let's see the English government protect you! Neutral waters or not, I am commander of this vessel. As regards you and Miss Vale, I shall do as I please here or elsewhere!"

He conducted them to Ethel's state-room and added:

"I will leave you here together for the present. I must now be prepared to take care of Capt. Willis when he makes his appearance!"

He left them, locking them up securely, having found the key in the door.

Mr. Vale flung himself on the low couch, and covered his face with his hands, moaning:

"Oh, my poor Ethel! I do not grieve for myself, but for you and Ned!"

The tears came to the poor girl's eyes, and it required all her self-control to prevent her giving way to sobs, but she exerted herself to comfort her father, seating herself upon his knees and smoothing his hair, drawing his hand from his face and kissing it tenderly, and in loving words and actions manifesting her affection for him.

"Perhaps, after all, dear father," she said, "Ned may return in company with a large number of the passengers and crew. In that case he would soon release us!"

Meantime, the villains had gone back to the forecastle to await the return of our hero. They had not waited long before a boat returned with a few of the passengers and seamen. As soon as they came on board they were seized and ironed, and confined in the hold under guard. They were hardly disposed of when another boat load of passengers, including several ladies, climbed up the sides of the vessel, and these were also secured without noise, and the men put into the hold, and the women taken to the cabin.

The glow of sunset had long since died away, and the shadows of evening were resting darker between the vessel and the shore, when Capt. Willis, attended by three or four seamen, carrying provisions, came on board.

He was instantly confronted by the villian and half a dozen of his men.

In the faint light of the rising moon, Capt. Willis instantly recognized his enemies, and drew his weapons.

"Surround him!" commanded Murlick. "Seize him, three at once, while the rest of you attend to the others!"

The order was obeyed. Three of the Confederates besides Murlick himself sprang upon our hero and endeavored to seize him. He fought desperately, killing one of his assailants and wounding the villain himself slightly in the shoulder, but he was at length secured and ironed. His men had already ceased their struggles, having been taken at a disadvantage, and were also secured.

Murlick then ordered Capt. Willis to be taken down to Ethel's state-room, he leading the way and unlocking the door.

The surprise and grief of the lovers at their strange meeting, can be better imagined than described.

Despite Ethel's entreaties, Mr. Vale was hand-cuffed and a ball and chain attached to his feet, and also one to Ned's.

"You may as well say good bye to each other now," said Murlick, in a brutal tone, "for it ain't very likely you'll see each other again soon, if ever!"

Ethel appealed to him, demanding what he meant, but received no reply, save a mocking and triumphant laugh.

Capt. Willis comprehended the awful malignity expressed in the villain's words and tone, and said:

"Come here, darling!"

Ethel went to him, and he whispered a few words of love and encouragement in her ear, kissing her and bidding her not to give way to despair. Ethel embraced him with a fervor that brought a diabolical scowl upon Murlick's face, and then went to her father.

"Come, hurry up!" said the Confederate. "You can say 'farewell forever,' in two words, as well as a hundred?"

He ordered his men to remove Capt. Willis to a state-room, and himself attended to locking him up securely. He then had Mr. Vale placed in another state-room and similarly secured, and returned to the half-fainting girl.

"As a special favor to you, my dear Ethel," he said, "I won't have you ironed or chained. I will take the precaution, however, of locking your door. Good night!"

He left her, locking the door behind him and carrying away the key, while the poor girl, moaning in anguish, flung herself on her couch and gave way to her grief.

Murlick returned to the deck and ordered all the prisoners in the hold to be taken ashore, ironed as they were, and gave the keys of their irons to one of the men whom he released. Thus, nobody was left on the bark save the Vales, our hero, and the Confederates. The villain then placed a guard in the cabin and went ashore.

In the course of an hour he returned.

"And now we'll go!" he said to his men. "Up with the anchor, boys, as quickly as possible, and let's be off!"

The order was obeyed, and the bark started out of the bay with a fair wind for the Indian Ocean.

The Confederates were jubilant.

"And now for a good sleep," muttered the villain, after he

had issued his orders for the night, and seen that his three prisoners were safe. "I am tired with my three days in a water cask!"

He retired to his state-room, in the happy conviction that he was master of the situation, and was soon heard snoring loudly. From the words he had addressed to the prisoners, and from his treatment of them, they well knew that a terrible darkness was before them.

"All is lost now!" moaned Ethel, as she gave way to a flood of tears, in her solitude. "O, father! what will become of us? O, Edward! Edward!"

The father and the lover, each in his own way, were oppressed by similar emotions. What a terrible night was that upon which they had entered!

CHAPTER IX.

A CRUEL SEPARATION.

The forebodings of the prisoners, respecting their future were too well-founded.

About the middle of the following forenoon, Murlick came to the door of the state-room in which Mr. Vale was confined, and looked in upon him, saying:

"Good morning, Mr. Vale, I'm sorry to have kept you waiting until now for your breakfast. The fact is, I overslept myself, having been thoroughly exhausted by the cares and anxieties of the past week!"

The merchant did not know what to make of these words, they were so much in contradiction to the villain's former manners towards him, and even to his present appearance. For a moment he hoped that reflection had inclined his enemy to mercy, but the next instant it occurred to him that this unnatural calmness and politeness preluded a worse evil than he had yet suffered.

"Breakfast?" repeated Mr. Vale, endeavoring to be calm.

No apology is necessary, Lieut. Murlick, on that score. I desire nothing to eat!"

"Nonsense—You have lost your spirits. I shall seek to restore them!"

He removed the ball and chain from his prisoner, and conducted him out of the state-room, seating him beside the table that occupied the centre of the cabin. Mr. Vale did not reply to his address, except with a sigh. Never, in his whole life, had the merchat seen an hour when his heart was more heavy. He had marked the blood-shot eyes of the villain, and the villainous satisfaction expressed on every feature, and noticed that he was somewhat affected by whiskey, his breadth fairly reeking with it.

"I am having a fine breakfast made ready for you," said Murlick, as he indicated the dishes placed on the table. "I will call your daughter, and we will have a sociable time together!"

He proceeded to Ethel's state-room, and invited her to appear, saying that Mr. Vale was waiting to see her. She joined her father with a sad but affectable greeting, and entered into conversation with him.

"My poor child!" the merchant soon exclaimed, reaking in upon some expression of consolation she was trying to impart to him. "It is killing me to see you suffer!"

They mingled their tears together.

"You did not sleep?" he continued.

"No. I could only think of you and Edward!"

Murlick turned away with a malignant scowl, Ethel having spoken in a tone too low to reach his hearing, and proceeded to relieve Capt. Willis of chain and ball, and conduct him to the table, with a singulated and hollow politeness.

"Now you must all be quiet, and make no effort to escape or otherwise annoy me," the villain then said. "It is clear that there is a difference of ideas and inclinations among us, but that is no reason why we should not eat breakfast so sociably together!"

He seated himself at the end of the table, with a bow of

mock politeness, while our hero and Ethel exchanged greetings.

"May I ask, Lieut. Murlick?" said Mr. Vale, after a pause, "what direction you are steering—where we are going?"

"Well, sir, to the best of my belief," replied the half-drunken villain, "we are steering northwest, and are bound for almost any destination to which I may be pleased to travel!"

Mr. Vale could not fully master his indignation at this response, and he accordingly said:

"You will yet see trouble, Lieut. Murlick, in the career upon which you have entered. You were sent by Captain Semmes to land us at the Cape, and you have no business, as a naval officer, to do anything more or less than your instructions command and warrant!"

The villain laughed jeeringly—insultingly.

"And do you really suppose that Capt. Semmes sent me to the Cape to land you and the rest of your Yankees?" he demanded, half arising. "Nothing of the kind. I came here to gain the latest information about the *Vanderbilt* and our other Federal pursuers, and also concerning some new war steamers that Capt. Semmes is daily expecting to report to him here. Land you, indeed! You must think a load of Yankees of some account, to suppose that twelve or fifteen of us would come all this way with you. No, sir, we came with the intention of going back in a swift steamer, if she had made her appearance. Had it not been for this, the prisoners would have been started off alone in the bark, to work their own way to port, as we have so often done by our prisoners heretofore!"

These confidences thoroughly exposed the character of the man and of the cause to which his services were devoted.

"Well be that as it may," responded Mr. Vale, "you have no business to treat us as you have done. It is not possible that Capt. Semmes, much less the so-called government you serve, can look approvingly upon such villainy as you have manifested towards my daughter, Captain Willis, and myself!"

"You are right, Mr. Vale—Capt. Semmes and the Confederate government would not look approvingly upon my conduct in this matter—and I will take good care that they do not look upon it at all, either approvingly or otherwise!"

A stern rebuke arose to the merchant's lips, but he did not utter it, a realization of his utter helplessness teaching him discretion. He partially subdued his emotion, by the exercise of his stern will, and then remarked:

"You choose to speak in enigmas, Lieut. Murlick!"

"Do I?" he responded, with an insulting laugh. "You will soon be able to read the riddle!"

One of his men appeared at this moment, bearing a large tray filled with refreshments, including almost everything that the well filled larder of a sea-captain can furnish. A pot of steaming coffee completed the repast, and yielded such an agreeable aroma to the air, that Mr. Vale and Capt. Willis felt their appetites returning to them, despite their sorrows.

Dismissing his servant—a volunteer from the forecastle—Murlick drew the several dishes around him, and commenced eating. Mr. Vale felt sick at heart as he comprehended that the villain had made such a pretense of giving his prisoners breakfast only to tantalize them.

"You can see that I have barely sufficient for one such hearty man as I am"; the villain remarked, pouring himself a cup of coffee. "I suspect that you will put on airs, if I feed you too well. It seems desirable to teach you, even through this despised medium, as well as in other ways, that I am the master of your several destinies!"

Chained as he was, Capt. Willis was sorely tempted to arise and seize his enemy. He had measured his strength and felt that he could strangle him with his fettered hands, but a timely realization of the horrible revenge the crew of the bark would wreak upon him and his companions, even in case of his success, caused him to dismiss the temptation.

Accordingly not a movement was made by the prisoners, nor a word uttered, while the ruffian ate his breakfast.

"There, I feel a little better!" finally declared Murlick, arising, "I am now prepared to attend to business!"

He called, and a couple of his men, with loaded pistols in their hands, came out of his state-room.

"You can go forward, boys," remarked Murlick to them, "and take this mess with you!"

The men vanished with the remains of his breakfast, and he then added:

"I put them there, as a precaution against any sudden outburst of rage on the part of any of you. That's all!"

He might have added that he had hoped, by his late tantalizing proceeding, to lead our hero into some act that would warrant him in calling his men and shooting him down on the spot. The patience and thoughtfulness of Capt. Willis had alone prevented this scheme from being carried out.

Murlick was silent a moment, lighting a cigar, and then he seated himself at the end of the table opposite his prisoners, and addressed them as follows:

"As indicated, I am now ready for business. I love your daughter, Mr. Vale, and wish to make her my wife, not only for her own intrinsic value, but as the easiest way of settling the old score that existed between us, years ago. You have probably learned by this time that I can be ugly, and you will probably not be surprised to hear that I ask her hand on a purely business basis. All of you are in my hands, and you can never regain your liberty except on such terms as I am pleased to grant—"

Say no more on this subject, Lieut. Murlick," interrupted Mr. Vale, with quiet firmness, although his face was deathly pale. "I would sooner see my child in her coffin, than give her to you in marriage. The more I have seen of you during the past week, the more firmly am I convinced that the destruction of one member of my family already rests at your door. I allude to my lost son—"

The awful look of triumph that lit up the savage face of Murlick, caused the merchant to pause.

A suppressed cry of horror escaped Ethel.

"It is clear," said Ned, with forced calmness, "that this man has, as we have all along suspected, the secret of the fate of Ethel's lost brother!"

"What folly is this?" exclaimed Murlick, after schooling his features and emotions to quietude, "You are talking of something that does not concern me, and that I do not understand. Let me bring you back to my proposition, Mr. Vale. If you will give me Ethel in marriage—for her own consent or non-consent I care nothing—I will forget all my past hatred, be friendly to you, give Capt. Willis his freedom, and make the girl a good husband. Refuse to give her to me, and I will set you both adrift, this night, in a boat, in mid-ocean, and hold the girl captive without any consent at all in the matter!"

This horrible threat brought Mr. Vale and Capt. Willis both to their feet, manacled as they were. Their eyes blazed and their forms shook with their emotions.

"I give you till to-night to consider the proposal," pursued Murlick, as he rolled his bloodshot eyes from one to the other. "In the meantime, you will do well to realize that I have a force at command to carry the alternative into execution. See here!"

He again called, and two more of his men completely armed, came out of his state-room, and stood awaiting his orders.

"Shut these prisoners up exactly as you disposed of them last night," he commanded, "and thereafter keep guard over them till further notice, looking in upon them every half-hour!"

The order was obeyed, and Murlick sauntered on deck.

The day wore slowly away, and night came on.

The sky was half hidden by scudding clouds, and everything threatened, at no distant period, a tempest.

At an early hour of the evening, the prisoners were taken on deck by several of the confederates, acting under Murlick's personal directions.

They found the bark hove to on the water.

A boat without oars, sails, or provisions, lay alongside.

"What is your decision, Mr. Vale?" asked the villain, in a hoarse whisper.

"The same as it was this morning, sir, I'd sooner see Ethel dead than give her to you! We'd all sooner be hung and quartered than consent to your wickedness! We leave ourselves and you to the God which is in heaven!"

"*Enough!*"

This was all that Murlick said.

Two of his men seized Ethel and held her motionless.

Four others seized Capt. Willis and Mr. Vale, and lowered them, bound and ironed, into the boat.

The line fastening the boat to the bark was severed.

The boat drifted away, disappearing in the darkness.

The bark resumed its course.

And a wild shriek of despair and horror burst from the lips of Ethel, and she sank fainting to the deck.

God of mercy! what a separation had come!

CHAPTER X.

TREACHERY.

A murmur of disapprobation came from the crew of the bark, after Murlick had thus disposed of Mr. Vale and Capt. Willis, and the villain called a couple of the grumbling seamen to him, saying:

"Here, if you are so tender-hearted, carry this girl down to the cabin and bring her to her senses!"

The men obeyed the order in silence, lifting Ethel carefully and carrying her to the cabin, where they bathed her face in cold water and chafed her hands, regarding her meanwhile with pitying looks.

The poor girl soon recovered her senses and started to her feet with a moaning cry.

kindly. "Make the best you can of your situation, Miss, and thank Providence 'tain't no worse!"

With this remark, meant to be consoling, he ushered her into her state-room, and, finding the key still in the lock, fastened her in.

The night was a long vision of horror to Ethel. The dashing of the waves against the vessel seemed to her like a requiem over the death of her loved ones, and again like mockings and rejoicings that struck a thrill of terror to her soul. Every breeze that filled the sails seemed to her laden with their dying moans, and several times she listened intently, thinking she heard them call her name. Her anguish was to deep for tears—she could only press her hands over her hot eye-balls and moan despairingly. At times, she paced her narrow floor wildly, and again she sank down upon her couch—motionless and apparently lifeless.

In the morning, Murlick sent her some bread and water, but she did not touch it.

The villain himself did not come near her during the forenoon, but once or twice sent a man with his compliments, and a request to know the state of her health.

In the afternoon the wind began to rise and soon increased into one of those short-lived but terrible gales, well-known to seamen in those latitudes. As Ethel heard the creaking of the ship and the crackling sound of the straining timbers, she could hardly repress a shriek.

To her tortured imagination was vividly presented the picture of that little oarless, sailless boat, with its two heavily ironed and helpless prisoners, tossing helplessly on the waters, or perhaps ere this engulphed in the yeast of waves.

The wind at length moderated, and then sounds of confusion was heard on the deck.

It was discovered that the bark had sprung a leak, and was rapidly filling.

"To the pumps!" shouted Murlick, as his men communicated the fearful discovery.

The men sprang to their work, but their efforts were unavailing. The water gained upon the pumps.

"Out with the boats!" then commanded Murlick. "We must abandon the bark, boys, and trust ourselves to luck. The water is getting calm. Be lively!"

The boats were lowed and filled with provisions; a compass and other necessary articles were stowed in them; and Murlick then went for Ethel. He ordered her trunk to be carried out, muttering:

"There's plenty of room for it, and it may conciliate her to have it taken along!"

The haggard face and wild eyes of the girl were noticed by the villain, but he felt no sorrow at the change his cruelty had wrought. The thought occurred to him, however, that she might attempt to jump overboard, and he therefore resolved to guard her closely. He handed her down into the boat, and then seated himself beside her, and the men pushed off.

They were still within a short distance of the bark, when they saw her make a sudden plunge forward, and then go down, disappearing completely from their view.

"Well, boys," said Murlick, looking back to the spot where the bark had been, "we'll keep our boats together, and perhaps get picked up to-morrow. If not, we have provisions enough to last until we can make some point on the African coast."

The boats kept together, and, the night being brilliant with moonlight and starlight, the men kept up their courage, singing songs and telling yarns. Ethel wrapped herself up in her shawl, and shaded her face with her straw gipsey hat and then, leaning over the side of the boat, gazed into the dark waters of the ocean with a strangely fixed gaze, as if expecting to see the ghastly faces of her loved ones.

All night she sat in the same position, sinking into a despairing apathy, and never once removing her gaze from the sea, and not even noticing the reflections of the moon and stars.

About the middle of the next forenoon, as they were

skimming along, with their sails spread to the light breeze. Murlick suddenly detected a sail to the southward, which threatened to cross their track. A flag of distress was instantly hoisted and was soon noticed, and in the course of half an hour or more, the party of ship-wrecked Confederates were taken on board of a first class ship.

Murlick instantly fabricated an affecting story of his wreck, and asked the commander his name and destination.

"My name is Morris," replied that officer—an intelligent looking man of middle age, with a benevolent expression of countenance—"and this is the brig *Mary Ball*, of New York, bound to Mauritius."

"We were bound to Manilla," replied Murlick, "and will pay you liberally for our passage to Mauritius, if you will take us."

"Certainly," replied Capt. Morris. "I would not be so inhuman as to set you again adrift. I will land you at Mauritius, and you can proceed thence anywhere you choose."

Ethel, who had been standing near the bulwarks, under guard, now scanned the face of the captain, and, feeling confidence in his goodness, as expressed in his face, said:

"May I have a moment's conversation with you, Capt. Morris?"

The captain regarded her pale and earnest face a moment, and came towards her, as he replied:

"Certainly Miss. Can I do anything for you?"

Ethel began to relate her persecutions by Murlick, and describe the horrible fate to which he had subjected her lover and father, when the wily villain interrupted her, saying quietly:

"Excuse me, Capt. Morris, for not introducing you to my sister before. She was accompanying me to Manilla, but, poor girl!" he added, with assumed grief, "our wreck and dangers have turned her brain—she has been wild and flighty all day—even refusing to call me brother!"

Capt. Morris expressed his grief at Ethel's afflictions, and, feeling reluctant to listen to the girl's supposed ravings, said:

"What is your name sir?"

"Oh—ah!" stammered the villain. "I am Horace Jones. of Portland!"

"Well, Mr. Jones, I will give you and your sister each a state-room, and will soon arrange accommodations for your men. We have a small crew and would be glad of their assistance for the short time they will be on board. Please follow me. Poor girl," he added, in a lower tone. "What horrible things she does imagine!"

Ethel saw that she had nothing to hope from another application to Capt. Morris, and therefore submitted quietly, when Murlick took her hand in a grasp and led her to the cabin. The captain assigned her a state-room, and the girl's trunk was placed in it, Murlick locking her up and following the captain to another.

"I believe you said you were short of hands," said the villain, carelessly, after inquiring the news. "You are welcome to the services of my men—and mine also, if necessary!"

"Oh, no!" returned Capt. Morris, unsuspiciously. "We have nine men, and yours in addition will give us a handsome complement. We left port with fifteen men, but it seems as if some strange fatality had followed us ever since. Six of the men have died of fever, fallen overboard, or met with some fatal accident, so that your arrival is a real godsend. I will have a good breakfast brought down to you and your sister," he added. "Poor child! What a pity it is necessary to lock her up!"

He left the cabin to give orders for a breakfast.

An infernal gleam of joy lighted up the villain's face, as he muttered:

"Only nine men on board! and I have eleven!"

A tempting breakfast was soon placed before Murlick, and he was left to himself to eat it. His first movement was to release Ethel and seat her beside him at the table.

"You must be pretty hungry by this time, my dear," he observed, as he began to carve the meat before him. "I hope your hunger will be the means of bringing you to terms."

"I do not wish for food," said Ethel, rejecting the plate he placed before her. "I can not eat!"

The villain paused and regarded her intently. As he observed how wan and deathly pale her face was, how thin she had grown in the last twenty-four hours, and how intensely mournful was the expression of her countenance, a sudden fear chilled him.

What if she were to die on his hands, and baulk thus his love for her and his hate for her father!

As hopeless as she was, it occurred to Ethel that it was a duty for her to try to partake of the food offered her, and she commenced eating, with the thought that her lot might yet be changed for the better.

"That's right!" said Murlick, in a milder tone, as he helped himself plentifully. "Always make the best of your situation, my dear Ethel, and yield gracefully to circumstances. By so doing, you will prolong your life and save yourself a great deal of trouble! There is no use in yielding so to grief at your loss. It is true that your father and Capt. Willis are food for fishes before this—I do not remind you of this to make you feel bad, but to let you see I am your only protector, and that the most sensible thing you can do is to conciliate me. You have realized by this time that I have power, and that I can use it. I am now going to lock you up and attend to a little business I have on hand!"

He conducted her back to her state-room and locked her in, and then sauntered out on deck, meeting Capt. Morris, and entering into conversation with him, after which he proceeded to look after his men.

His wicked brain had conceived a daring and infamous plot—that of rewarding the kindness of his host with a fearful treachery!

He had resolved to capture the vessel, and take her captain and crew prisoners!

He soon placed himself in communication with his men, and made known to them his plan. He assured himself that they were thoroughly armed, and then told them to be in readiness for his signal, which would be given at the most favorable moment.

That moment soon arrived.

When the captain and his mate were at dinner in the cabin and entertaining their guest with anecdotes and every evidence of honest hearted hospitality, Murlick arose from his seat, at the same moment that three of his men entered displaying their weapons, and ordered them to surrender to the officers of the Confederate States.

"Not a word—not a breath!" he said, placing his pistol to the head of Capt. Morris. "At the first sound, I'll blow your brains out!"

Two of the men were offering similar arguments to the mate, and the officers, being defenceless, surrendered. They were speedily bound with ropes, which were found in one of the state-rooms, and gagged and stowed away.

Murlick and his men then went on deck.

The man at the wheel was secured without a struggle, his suprise at the manifestations of the new passengers rendering him speechless.

The confederates then proceeded to the forecastle and surprised the crew eating dinner. The surprise was so complete, that there was little or no resistance to the menacing weapons of the assailants, and they were speedily placed in a powerless condition, under guard, in the hold.

Murlick then rubbed his hands jubilently.

"Well done, boys," he said. "We will not steer for the Dodo islands!"

He placed one of his men at the wheel, and entered into formal possession of the vessel, examining the brig's papers, hunting for the money with which Capt. Morris proposed to purchase his cargo, and eventually finding it. His prize put him in the best of spirits, and he resolved to say nothing to the crew in regard to the money, but divide it with Semmes, seeing that his superior officer could not fail to detect that it was in his possession.

During the three or four days that followed his capture

of the brig, Lieut. Murlick left Ethel to herself, sending her meals regularly to her and once or twice forcing her to eat at his table. He did not, however, annoy her with protestations of his love, and a sentiment of fear began to mingle with his love for her, as he marked the unearthly brightness of her eyes and increasing pallor of her sweet young face.

On the fourth morning after taking the brig, Murlick arrived in sight of a group of low islands, covered with trees, and he stood at the wheel as the vessel was turned into a narrow and deep channel between the two largest of the group.

He suddenly descried a small picket-boat as it darted into a channel leading into a lagoon, and immediately shouted to the boatman, giving his name.

The brig was then turned into a narrow channel revealed, and her crew thronged the deck. At the same moment was revealed to their gaze the *Alabama*, disguised in a new coat of paint, lying idly in a small inland lagoon, surrounded on every side by trees.

The picket preceded the new comers, and, when they had rounded to beside the steamer, Capt. Semmes was waiting on his deck, surrounded by his crew, to receive them.

Murlick instantly went on board the *Alabama*, going to the cabin with Semmes, where they remained closeted nearly an hour When at length they emerged on deck, there was a satisfied expression on the countenance of the pirate chief that was due to Murlick's promise of dividing with him his spoils. The villain ordered his prisoners to be brought on board the steamer, and Capt. Morris and his men were stowed away, the former with his mate in a stateroom, the latter in the hold.

Ethel was then brought to Semmes's vessel.

The pirate chief could not resist a wondering exclamation, as he noticed the difference suffering had wrought in the maiden's looks since she had left his vessel.

Ethel made an effort to appeal to him.

"I know all about it," said Semmes, soothingly. "I've heard the whole story!"

"Oh, no--you have not!" said the poor girl. "Let me tell you——"

"I beg you to make your statement to Lieut. Murlick," interrupted Semmes. "He is the executive officer of the vessel. He will take good care of you, my dear young lady, so have no fears. You will please excuse me now, as I am really very busy!"

Thus dismissed, Ethel sorrowfully followed a guard to the cabin and discovered that she was not only allowed a state-room but free range of the cabin.

Murlick had related to his superior officer a fictitious story to the following effect. He stated that his prisoners had in some way freed themselves and arisen on the voyage to the Cape; that he had hidden himself in a water cask; had a day or two later rescued his men in the most heroic manner; had provisioned a bark, and were about to embark—it being useless to attempt to regain the bark—when Ethel had appeared on deck. He had added that the girl was about to give the alarm and rouse the Yankees, and that he had seized her for his own safety and the safety of his men, and brought her with him to protect himself. He had then given a brief account of taking the brig, and was complimented by Semmes for his action.

Thus, Ethel was completely in the toils of her enemy.

The treasure stolen from the brig was brought on board the steamer and divided equally between Semmes and Murlick. The brig was then cleared of her valuables, and Semmes said:

"The steamer is ready to start immediately on a new cruise Lieut. Murlick. We will take the brig with us, and burn her to-night, on the open sea!"

The arrangements for departure were speedily made, the anchor weighed and the vessels stood away from the islands, into the open ocean.

The pirate was again looking for her prey; and at night, Semmes again lighted up his track with a conflagration.

CHAPTER XI.

UNBIDDEN GUESTS!

Capt. Willis and Mr. Vale tossed helplessly all night on the ocean.

How they suffered!

They said nothing to each other of Ethel's fate, that subject being too horrible for them to approach.

A couple of hours after daylight they were picked up by an American ship bound to Calcutta.

They explained their misfortunes sufficiently, their irons were stricken off, and they were kindly cared for, the commander of the ship being whole-souled.

For several days the ship continued her course without the occurrence of any event of importance, and then, one day, about noon, a steamer was seen in the distance.

It was at once suspected that she was a pirate.

She stood towards the ship.

The ship spread all her canvass in flight.

The steamer gained rapidly upon her, and finally displayed the confederate flag, firing again as a signal for the chase, to heave her to.

The signal was not obeyed.

The pursuer came nearer and nearer, and fired another shot which passed through the ship's main-topsail.

It was now conceded that the steamer was the *Alabama*.

"It's of no use to run," said the commander of the chase to his anxious guests." I am sorry you are falling into confederate hands again, but there is no help for it. We can't get away—may as well surrender—may get borded!"

He ordered his mate to heave to.

"Well, do not say anything to Capt. Semmes about us," said our hero, after a hurried colloquy with Mr. Vale. "We will delay our return to the steamer's prison as long as we can. We will hide in the hold of your ship, and you need not mention our presence!"

"Agreed, and success to you! Perhaps you can get up a raft, and steal away in the darkness!"

The sails of the ship flapped in the wind.

Capt. Willis and Mr. Vale had scarcely concealed themselves down deep in the hold of the ship, when Capt. Semmes reached her deck, at the head of half a dozen of his followers.

"Who commands this vessel?" he demanded.

The commander presented himself.

"Let me see your papers!"

The papers were produced and examined.

"I see," commented Semmes. "You are a Yankee, as I expected!"

He took possession of the vessel, with his usual formula, announcing his own name and that of the steamer.

"I hope you will bond the vessel, Capt. Semmes," said the helpless commander, "and allow me to proceed on my voyage. It can do you no good to burn her!"

Semmes shook his head and laughed.

"That bond business is used up," he said. "We can collect our claims, of course, at some future time, but I prefer to strike a present blow at your commerce. I don't take bonds any more, or I should be happy to oblige you. I shall burn your vessel to night. What is the number of your crew?"

The commander informed him.

"Any passengers?"

"We did not take a single one, sir!"

"Umph! Please come aboard with me, and bring your chronometer. It will make the two hundred and eleventh of these instruments I have captured since leaving Mobile!"

It was now near the close of day.

The crew of the ship was transferred to the steamer, as were such parts of her outfit and cargo as the Confederates desired.

The crew was shut up in the hold, and the commander and his mates were assigned quarters in the cabin, and given the freedom of the deck.

The water being smooth, the ship was made fast to the *Alabama*, and both lay quiet on the waters, Semmes being desirous of saving his coal, and thinking that he might as well await his prey there as elsewhere.

The few goods desired by the captors were soon removed to the steamer, and a dreary solitude settled around the spot in which Mr. Vale and Capt. Willis were hidden.

"They'll burn the ship soon after dark," said Mr. Vale; "and we must change our quarters to the steamer. I wish to see if Murlick has come back."

"If he has," responded Capt. Willis, in a tone of implacable resolve, "we may at least punish him for his deeds."

"Yes. Perhaps he brought Ethel back with him. Perhaps if we succeed in getting aboard the steamer unseen, we may be able to effect her rescue!"

They discussed the perils and prospects of the proposed movement, and determined to enter upon it soon after nightfall.

"The most of the sailors won't know but that we belong to the last vessel captured," said Ned, after a long and thoughtful silence. "I think we can effect our transfer unnoticed!"

They made their way to the deck.

The crew of the *Alabama* was busy, flying to and fro, and making preparations to burn the prize.

The two men saw that they had not started an instant too soon.

Some of the Confederates leaped from the steamer to the deck of the ship.

"Now's our time," whispered Ned to Mr. Vale, as a friendly cloud momentarily obscured the light of the moon "Come!"

He climbed to the deck of the steamer assisting Mr. Vale to follow him.

They were seen, of course—but the observers supposed

that they belonged to the crew of the steamer—to the party of burners.

The men who had boarded the ship were accumulating combustibles to fire her.

The remainder of the watch were preparing the *Alabama* to haul off from her decoy, into the surrounding darkness.

Capt. Semmes and Lieut. Murlick were both busy, moving about and giving orders.

Slouching their hats and turning away their faces, the two intruders glided across the deck quietly, and made their way down into the lower hold, where they concealed themselves among boxes and bales, much as Murlick had hidden himself on board the bark.

"Thank God!" ejaculated Mr. Vale, in a voice husky with grateful emotion. "We are here undetected? They do not know of our presence!"

Ned pressed his hand warmly.

"Perhaps Ethel was brought here, he said. "We may yet be able to communicate with her, and even bear her away with us'"

"Oh! if we could do so—if I could once more see you together safe and happy—I could die without a murmur!"

"Let us be strong and hope for the best. It is a great encouragement that we are here unbidden guests in their midst."

"Yes. But what shall be our next move?" responded Mr. Vale. "Our object is to see if Ethel is here, to see if we can rescue her, to punish Murlick, and to investigate the resemblance borne me by that midshipman."

Ned started, and a flush appeared on his face.

"I had not thought of him," he said. "My mind was elsewhere—but he's the very man to aid us in this extremity."

"Do you think so?"

"I know it. Let him be who or what he will, I know that he will not turn a deaf ear to our wrongs and suffering. I had but a passing glimpse of his face, but I saw enough of him in that moment to know that he is out of place here. He has the only prepossessing countenance that I have seen among the officers and crew of this vessel!"

Mr. Vale choked down the wild hopes which had momentarily thrilled him, and asked:

"You think then, that we had better make an effort to see this midshipman, as our first move?"

"Yes. I will leave you here, and go on deck. I had better go, instead of you, there being more men about my size and height than of yours. You must keep up your courage. I will do all that I can do. Let us hope in God's mercy."

He wrung the hand of the merchant with a feeling expression of affection, and hurried to the deck!

CHAPTER XII.

THE MYSTERIOUS MIDSHIPMAN.

The ship had been fired in several places and was now in flames, throwing a red glare far over the waters.

The steamer had withdrawn beyond the circle illuminated by it, and lay quiet in the darkness.

The greater portion of the crew had collected on the bow of the *Alabama* and were looking towards the burning vessel.

Casting a sharp glance around, Ned was gratified to see the object of his search at no great distance, leaning over the bulwarks amidships and gazing abstractedly into the sea.

It struck Ned as something singular that his face was turned away from the burning ship, and that his attitude was one of dejection.

Noticing that he stood alone, the young captain glided towards him without attracting the attention of the confederates, and laid his hand on his arm.

The midshipman started, and uttered an exclamation.

"Hush!" said Ned, in a low tone. "Do not call attention! I would like to speak with you confidentially a few minutes—"

"Certainly," replied the midshipman, politely. "Will you come to my state-room? I suppose you are one of the new prisoners. If I can do anything for you, I shall be glad to know it!"

"I will remain here, if you please," replied Ned, looking cautiously around him. May I ask your name?"

"It is James Murlick."

"You are then, the son of Lieut. Murlick?"

"Yes," replied the young man, after a moment's hesitation—

This statement was followed by an awkward pause, during which our hero regarded his companion narrowly, looking in vain for some resemblance to the villain.

In the clear moonlight he noticed the young man's slight figure, his frank boyish face, with its broad high brow, its clear dark eyes, and general expression of nobleness and manliness.

"Can it be?" he asked himself. "This youth has not a point of resemblance to the lieutenant—is noble and good, I am sure! There must be some mystery here! The best way to awaken his confidence is to be confidential!"

He determined to appeal to the midshipman in plain and direct terms.

"Let me tell you who and what I am" he said, aloud, glancing around him as he spoke, and assuring himself that the officers and crew were all absorbed in watching the burning craft. "My name is Willis—I was captain of the *Ocean Cloud* destroyed by Semmes two weeks ago—"

The midshipman uttered an exclamation, and regarded our hero with interest, appearing to call him to his memory.

Ned then went on to state the events that had followed his capture, told of Mr. Vale and his daughter, and their persecutions by Murlick, and detailed everything, as briefly as possible, up to the moment of his present interview with the midshipman. The interest of the listener in the narration was intense, and when the narrator had concluded, the youth's face expressed the utmost horror.

"And this is the man I have called father!" he said, with

a singular agitation. "His cruelty is even greater than I knew or imagined."

He was silent a moment, struggling with his emotions, and then continued:

"Let me respond to your confidences, Capt. Willis, with my own history—that is, if it will not trouble you to listen to it. I promise not to detain you long!"

"I desire nothing better than to hear your history!" responded Capt. Willis. "I have a greater desire to know it than you can imagine!"

The young man looked surprised, and our hero added.

"I will explain when you have finished!"

The midshipman flashed a quick glance around him, noticing that, though one or two of the seamen were crossing the deck, he and his visitor were unnoticed. The ship was now a mass of flames, so that almost every eye was riveted upon it, or looking eagerly for prey.

"The first I remember," began the youth, in a tone of emotion, "I was living with a couple of poor whites, near New Orleans. They were completely ignorant and degraded, being lower in intelligence than any negro I ever met, oppressed with poverty and wretchedness, and by no means honest. When I was five or six years old, I remember that my father—Abner Murlick—came to see me, and appeared pleased with my appearance, which must have been more or less like my companions. That was the first time I ever remembered to have seen him. The people with whom I lived, had told me that he brought me to them when I was little more than a year old. He gave them a scanty pittance for taking care of me, and enjoined them to bring me up in their habitual filth and ignorance!"

Ned expressed his surprise.

"But his designs were providentially frustrated," continued the midshipman. "When I was about six years old, I had the good-fortune to attract the attention of a kind city missionary, by some exhibition of childish wit, and he immediately had me suitably clothed and sent to school, where I rapidly progressed. The people with whom I lived, soon looked up to me, regarding me as a superior being. The man died, and I found it easy enough to get along with the woman, even exciting her pride to keep clean and honest. I was soon beyond the common school in which I had been placed, and the kind missionary enlisted some friends in my behalf, and sent me to a first-class high-school. When I next saw my father I was sixteen, well-dressed, versed in the languages, mathematics and current literature, and fond of study. He was disappointed in me. His rage was awful. He had wished me to grow up in ignorance and vice, and fairly raved at the woman in whose charge he had put me. I have never known what to make of his conduct at that time. He immediately removed me from school, and kept me awhile with him, finally insisting, after the out-breaking of the war, on my becoming a middy on board the *Alabama*, to which he had himself been appointed. Again, then, was a bitter scene between us. My heart was with the North—perhaps from the fact that my kind friend, the missionary, was a Northerner. I refused at first to join the Confederates, but a variety of circumstances induced me to re-consider my refusal. In the first place, I could not make my way North. In the second, Lieut. Murlick—for I cannot call him father—threatened to denounce me as a traitor, and have me arrested. Filial duty, a hope of mitigating the hardships of prisoners, etc., did the rest, and I consented. Since then, he has kept me almost constantly under his own eyes, treating me as though he hated me, and often I have encountered such looks in his eyes as have almost caused me to fear him."

He paused, as Ned looked around, but the pirates were still engaged at the end of the vessel, and he continued:

"Putting the various facts of his conduct towards me together, and remembering his horrible barbarity in wishing to bring me up in ignorance and wickedness, I have lately concluded that there is a mystery in the matter—that he hates me—that I am not his son!"

Capt. Willis was even more agitated at the youth's words than the midshipman himself.

"You are right!" he said. "I do not believe that you are his son. It seems to me that he has stolen you from an enemy, proposing to wreak a horrible revenge by making a brute of you!"

"Stolen me!" repeated the youth. "Perhaps you are right. Everything in my history, as far as he is concerned, goes to confirm your idea! Do you know anything about it? Your manner seems to indicate that you do!"

"It is possible that I have a clue to the secret. You saw my friend, Mr. Vale. Years ago he married the girl whom Murlick loved, but who rejected him, and their first child, a boy named Eugene, was stolen from them. They suspected Murlick, owing to threats he had circulated against them. That boy would be twenty years old now—just your age— and your singular resemblance to Mr. Vale, confirms my hope and belief that you are his missing son!"

The youth's agitation was excessive.

"Is it possible?" he ejaculated, "Oh, I pray your words may be true! I can imagine no joy equal to that of having an honorable and loving father!"

"In that case," proceeded Ned, "your real name is Eugene Vale, and you have not only a father but a lovely sister. The young girl, Ethel Vale, whom you saw with us——"

Ned was interrupted, not only by his own griefs, and the thoughts that thronged upon him in relation to his betrothed, but by his companion's emotion,

"And that young girl, who so excited my sympathy, finally ejaculated the youth—" who is now mourning in her stateroom is, perhaps, my own sister! What joy to prove your suspicions true, Capt. Willis!"

The young captain turned deathly pale, as these words fell on his ears. His brain fairly reeled.

"Ethel in the cabin?" he ejaculated. "Is she, then, indeed, so near me?"

The midshipman instantly comprehended the state of affairs between the young couple, and went on to tell of Murlick's arrival with the girl, and the story with which he explained her presence. He then recalled the attention of our hero to himself.

"If I were really the lost son of Mr. Vale," he said, "how could he ever know it? Is there any way by which he could ever really decide the fact, beyond all cavil?"

"There is. He spoke to me of a mark on his son's arm, by which he should know him, were he ever to meet him!"

"A mark on his arm!" repeated the youth, fairly reeling, while his face became deathly pale. "Oh, heaven! I have such a mark!"

"You have? All these circumstances point to the fact that you are the missing son of Mr. Vale, for whom he has sorrowed so many years. You bear a singular resemblance to him, and the more I see of you the more you remind me of him—your very manner and voice seeming like his. I cannot resist the conviction—"

"Hush! Lieut. Murlick is approaching!" whispered the midshipman, hearing the familiar step of the lieutenant on the deck. "Lean over the bulwarks and look at the water. I'll be with you again in ten minutes!"

"He stepped away from Ned and met Murlick.

"I wish to see you, James," said the lieutenant, with a sharp glance at Ned, who had obeyed the middy's suggestion, and was looking into the water with his back to the newcomer.

The youth followed Murlick to the cabin, and our hero waited patiently for his return. His thoughts were busy with his betrothed, with the midshipman and with the patient and suffering father in the hold.

An hour glided away, and still the youth did not return. The decoy ship was burning down close to the water's edge, and the crew of the pirate, disappointed of their expected prey, were preparing to turn in. And still Ned stood unnoticed and overwhelmed with fearful forebodings at the steamer's side.

He waited another hour—a third—and still he saw no sign of the midshipman. Horrible anxieties came over him. He dared not linger longer where he was, lest he should attract attention. Sick at heart he returned to Mr. Vale.

CHAPTER XIII.

THE MIDSHIPMAN INVESTIGATES MATTERS.

Murlick led the way towards the cabin, followed by the midshipman, after the interview of the latter with Ned, as recorded.

Suddenly, the youth paused.

"One word, Lieut. Murlick," he said, "before we proceed further. I wish to ask you a question!"

Murlick started, and regarded him with an air of mingled surprise and inquiry.

"What do you mean, James?" he inquired. "Why don't you call me father, as usual?"

The youth hesitated a moment and then said:

"I will tell you why. It is because I am not certain that you bear that relationship to me, sir!"

Murlick looked at him with a face of blank amazement.

"Not certain that I am your father?" he stammered. "I think, James, that you must have broken your puling temperance pledge, and got tipsey! You had better clear your head of such nonsense as quickly as possible!"

"Excuse me, sir," replied the midshipman, quietly, but firmly. "You have never treated me as a father would a son, and I have reflected much on the subject lately—"

"Indeed!" sneered Murlick. "What conclusion did you arrive at!"

"That you are not my father, and that you bear some grudge against me!" was the frank reply, "I wish to know who I am—how I came in your hands—why you have so long ill-treated me, and who my parents are!"

Murlick's face grew almost black with rage.

"I don't know where you picked up all this romantic nonsense," he said, "but if you need my declaration that you are my son, you can have it! We will leave any further discussion on this subject to some future time. I have now something for you to do!"

He led the way to his state-room, the middy following, and then said:

"Here is some copying for you to do. I am going in to see Capt. Semmes, and expect to have it completed by my return."

He indicated a quantity of paper on the table, and then left the youth to his duty, which was one to which he was accustomed, he copying all the papers entrusted to him by Murlick for that purpose.

He was dissatisfied at the result of his interview with his pretended father, and his suspicions were confirmed that he was not his son.

As he seated himself at his appointed work, with the intention of hastening his return to Capt. Willis, the sounds of low sobbing fell on his ears. It evidently came from an adjacent state-room.

"Ah! the daughter!" he ejaculated, starting to his feet. "The poor girl is weeping over the supposed death of her father and lover. I must relieve her on that point and prepare her to see them and escape with them!"

He drew the key out of the lock of his state-room, and crossed the deserted cabin, unlocking her door, and entering her presence.

He closed the door behind him.

Slight as was the sound he made in doing so, the girl was aroused and lifted her head from its bowed position on the little table.

The midshipman was startled by the unearthly beauty of her face, her luminous eyes and deathly pale countenance being fully revealed in the dim light of a lantern hanging on her wall.

She looked at him in astonishment.

"Hush, lady!" whispered the youth. "Do not speak loud enough to betray my presence here!"

"You are a midshipman," said Ethel, looking at his uniform. "Father told me about you—about your strange resemblance to him. How strange!"

She had instantly detected his strange likeness to her father and looked at him attentively.

"Lady, setting aside all questions of this kind," he said, "let me proceed to more important matters. I have news for you. Be calm! You think your father and Capt. Willis dead—"

"Oh, yes!" she whispered, eagerly, looking widely at the youth. "Are they not dead? Do you know anything about them?"

Taking the girl's hand quietly in his own, he replied, in a tone of cordial kindness:

"No, they are not dead. They are safe on board this very steamer!"

A sudden light irradiated the girl's countenance, and she gave way to her wild emotion. The tears that had refused to flow in all her terrible anguish, now burst forth freely, relieving her brain of the fearful pressure it had sustained, and easing her oppressed heart.

"Are they prisoners?" she asked, as soon as she could command her voice.

"Not exactly," answered the youth, his own eyes moist with witnessing her joy. "They've stolen aboard from a captured vessel. We have hopes of effecting your escape, by and by, when all gets still for the night. Have patience, and do not get alarmed about your friends. They will be very cautious, so that you need have no fears! In the meantime, you will feel better to have this key by which you can leave this apartment at any moment. Take and keep it!"

"Is your own door unlocked?" asked Ethel, taking the instrument and putting it in her pocket.

"Yes. And now I must leave you. I expect to be interrupted every instant. Do not take any measure till you see me again!"

Repeating his encouraging remarks to her, and telling her to lock herself in, the youth returned to his writing.

His task was hardly completed when Murlick came in.

"I have been talking to Capt. Semmes about you," said the villain, after examining the young man's work, "and you will consider yourself under arrest, till further notice. If you can't remember that I am your father, sir, you *shall* remember that I am your superior officer!"

"Under arrest?" repeated the midshipman.

"Yes. Go to your quarters, and remain there till further orders!"

Without a word, but with a proud and defiant look, the midshipman went to his quarters and shut himself in.

"I'll stay here till Murlick goes to bed," he muttered, "and then sally forth. I must and will aid those prisoners, whether there is anything in all these suspicions of relationship, or not. This night shall see them out of this steamer and beyond the power of that bad man!"

CHAPTER XIV.

THE MIDNIGHT FLIGHT.

Capt. Willis found Mr. Vale almost wild with anxiety and apprehension, on returning to him.

"I feared that you were captured," he whispered—"did not know but you were dead. Oh! what waiting and watching!"

Ned stated that he had had a similar experience, and hastened to narrate all he had heard and seen, Mr. Vale listening with the greatest interest.

"Strange that he did not come back to you!" the merchant commented. "What can have happened? Can it be that his dealings with you were discovered? Is it possible that he has betrayed you?"

"No. He is noble and honest, and thoroughly devoted to us. I will answer for his good faith, with my life. My explanation of his non-return is that his lukewarmness in the Confederate cause has brought suspicion upon him, and that he has been arrested on some charge or another."

The merchant groaned.

"Then we are left to our own resources," he said, moaningly. "It is something, however, to know that Ethel is here. In regard to the question of his identity with my lost son, what is your opinion?"

Ned hesitated a moment, and then said:

"Perhaps I had better not answer your inquiry, Mr. Vale. We are in great trouble; everything seems uncertain; and perhaps——"

"I insist on an answer, Ned," interrupted Mr. Vale. "You have seen this young stranger, and have had an opportunity of forming a trustworthy opinion on this matter. Speak frankly to me, Ned—I can bear it!"

"I think, then, that this same young midshipman is your lost boy—your Eugene!"

For a moment the listener seemed strangling with the emotions this declaration caused him.

"Have you no doubts on the subject?"

"Not one. Everything points him out as the missing son, even as everything points at Murlick as his abductor."

Mr. Vail struggled with his emotions a moment in silence and then said:

"How we are placed, if your impression is the truth. All of us in the power of one foe—brother, sister, intended son-in-law, and father! Strange! strange!"

Ned echoed the sentiments, adding:

"And perhaps all these events have been providentially ordered by the Great Master of events, to restore your lost son to you! At least, we will hope for the best. The Confederates are now dismissing all hopes of being favored with a prize to-night, and in the course of an hour or two all will be still. We must wait till that time, and then make an attempt to communicate with Ethel. Since the midshipman knows where we are hiddden, he is liable to appear here any moment."

"Yes. Let us wait awhile in patience for his coming!"
Another hour passed.

"I am afraid that something serious has happened to our young friend," Ned finally observed. "I will slip up to the deck and reconnoitre."

He did so. He found the deck unusually quiet, the watch being gathered forward and remaining inactive.

He peered into the cabin, and saw Capt. Semmes and Lieut. Murlick seated by a table and conversing with each other.

He had regarded them but a moment, when they arose and came on deck.

He crouched under the bulwarks, watching them, and keeping perfectly still.

"We will lie quiet till morning, Murlick," observed Semmes. "We must be saving of our coal, or we shall get out before we make port. After all, perhaps we shall encounter a vessel just as soon where we are as to be steaming at full speed!"

Exactly. We are now in the usual track of East-Indiamen, and may soon have a prize."

The two men conversed a few moments longer, speaking about the weather, their prospects, etc., and then returned to the cabin. Ned understood that they were about retiring for the night, and a gleam of hope flashed into his mind.

He hurried back to Mr. Vale.

"We had better wait awhile," he whispered. "Our presence here is still unknown to Murlick, and he and Semmes are just turning in; perhaps our young friend is waiting for that event, and if so, he will soon be with us!"

They waited as patiently and hopefully as they could—yet in what restleness and anguish!

And while they waited, the object of their hopes—the young midshipman, was not idle.

He had been seated just inside the door of his state-room, waiting for Murlick and Semmes to turn in.

Knowing that Capt. Willis must be in great distress on account of his non-return, his own distress became great.

The two worthies at last retired to their quarters, and the watcher uttered a sigh of relief.

"Now to return to Capt. Willis," he thought. "And I will take the girl with me!"

He had in his room a dark lantern which he lighted and concealed under his coat. Securing his pistols, he cautiously opened his door and took a survey of the deserted cabin.

"There's risk, of course," he thought. "But I'll meet it!"

In a moment he was at Ethel's door, tapping lightly upon it, and keeping a sharp lookout around him.

The maiden answered his summons.

She had donned her cloak and hat, and had a small bundle of clothing in her hand, ready for flight.

"Come," he whispered, "Courage!"

He locked her door, and conducted her, half-carrying her at times, to the hold.

As the sound of their footsteps fell on the hearing of Capt. Willis and Mr. Vale, the latter nearly fainted.

"Do you hear, Ned?" he whispered. "The rustling of a dress!"

The midshipmen opened his lantern and set it on the head of a barrel, and then, holding the hand of the trembling girl, he said:

"Here, Capt. Willis! I have brought the young lady with me!"

The lover and father sprang to their feet.

Sobbing with joy, Ethel was clasped in the arms of her loved ones, and a wild scene of re-union followed.

When the first emotions of the meeting had subsided, and while Ethel's head was pillowed on the breast of her lover, and she was listeninng to his whispered words of love, Mr. Vale turned his attention to the middy.

"I thank you more than I can express for your kindness to me," he said, "in restoring my daughter. May you be rewarded a thousand fold!"

"I have already had my reward," returned the youth, "in witnessing your happiness!"

Mr. Vale turned the lantern in such a way as to distinctly

reveal their faces to each other, and he then looked long and earnestly at the middy, with marked emotion.

The youth himself scrutinized the face of the merchant, and felt his heart leap towards him with a sudden thrill of affection, such as he had never known.

"Capt. Willis has told me of your history," at length said Mr. Vale, in tremulous tones. "You have believed yourself the son of Abner Murlick, but he was not married twenty years ago! My heart tells me you are my son. If so, the fact can easily be proven. My boy had a natural mark on his arm, a distinct crescent. Have you any such peculiarity?"

He waited in breathless suspense for a reply.

Ethel and her lover watched the scene anxiously.

As fast as his trembling hands would permit, the youth pushed up his sleeve—revealing a blood-red crescent on his arm.

With a wild sob of joy, Mr. Vale caught him in his arms, pressing a father's kisses on his face, and receiving the boy's tender and loving caresses.

"My son, my son!" he murmured, straining him to his breast. "Found at last!"

His joy was too great for expression.

"When, at length, he released his son from his embrace, Ethel stood ready and anxious to greet her brother with all a sister's fond affection.

Capt. Willis and the middy then shook hands.

"Strange! strange!" ejaculated Mr. Vale, whose face was wet with tears of happiness. "After all these years, to find him in this way! It was indeed providential that we were captured by Semmes! It is singular," he added, "that we four—comprising our entire family—should be in the hands of Murlick!"

"We must not be in his hands long," said Ned. "We must be off from the steamer, within an hour. We must get a boat—"

"That is impossible," said the new-found son. "The boats

are all taken in from the davits and padlocked every night, to prevent them from being too handy to our prisoners!"

"What can we do, then, my son?" asked Mr. Vale.

"We must get up some kind of a float," was the reply. "I have been thinking of it this evening, and have devised a plan. There are a large number of india rubber floats aboard, which we can fasten together and use as a raft. It will be the best thing in the word for our use, since it is impossible to procure a boat! I will bring them down here, and we can prepare a raft from them."

As he concluded, he left them, but he soon returned with a large armful of floats, which they all proceeded to inflate, and which presented a formidable pile when fully distended.

"This will do for a basis," young Vale then declared, "We'll launch it, and build upon it!"

Aided by Capt. Willis, he carried the floats to the deck, arranged them into the shape of a parallelogram, with the aid of several spars, oars and other pieces of timber, which came opportunely to his hands. This labor was performed in a few minutes under cover of the darkness.

"Over with her!" whispered Eugene, with the sweat of toil and anxiety bathing his face. "We must hurry!"

By the exertion of their united strength, the two men launched their bulky float—or rather the skeleton and foundation of the raft they were intent on having.

"Go down to her, if you please, Capt. Willis," whispered Eugene. "Quick! an officer of the watch is coming."

Capt. Willis lowered himself by a rope to the raft.

The officer referred to sauntered near.

"What's going on here?" he asked.

"Executing orders," replied Eugene. "You need not trouble yourself about us, sir!"

The officer was Eugene's inferior in rank, but he resumed his way muttering, and entered the cabin.

"Now then," said young Vale to our hero, "I will pass you a huge pile of these floats, a plenty of ropes, some boards and timbers, which have been used by the painters and others, and also some provisions. The water is still, and we can blow up the floats and strengthen the concern, after we get safely off on it!"

They worked industriously ten minutes. Capt. Willis then declared the raft ready for its occupants.

"All right!" responded Eugene, "I will go for my father and sister!"

He hurried away, and soon conducted Mr. Vale and Ethel to the deck, and lowered them in safety to the raft.

"Now for some provisions!" he said. "Keep quiet a moment and I'll be with you!"

He hurried to the hold.

He had scarcely gone when a dark and malignant face looked over the bulwarks, and a hand was placed on the rope that held the raft to the steamer.

The fugitives looked up and (by the outlines of his head and shoulders against the sky) recognized Murlick!

The suspicious officer of the watch had called him.

"You'd better come back now!" he said, jeeringly. "I came out just in time to stop your little operations, I see. Ah!"

His eyes flamed with infernal joy as he noticed Mr. Vale, who had until then escaped his view, he seeing at first only Ethel and Capt. Willis.

"Plenty of accommodations on board," he added, drawing the rope closer. "We really can't spare you, my dear Ethel, and shall be only too glad, gentlemen, to have you return and tell us the secret of your marvellous escape and how you happen to be here. Come right up—or shall I call my men to assist you?"

Ethel trembled and would have fainted but for the reassuring pressure of her lover's arm.

Mr. Vale was overcome with horror.

At that moment, Eugene made his appearance, with a keg of water and a cask of sea-biscuit.

Murlick turned and saw him.

The midshipman relinquished his kegs.

"Treachery, eh?" exclaimed Murlick.

He had not time to say more, for Eugene promptly dealt him a sudden and heavy blow on the head with the barrel of his navy seven-shooter, and he reeled and fell senseless.

The midshipman then lowered the kegs to Capt. Willis, and descended to the raft, cutting the rope and pushing away from the steamer.

"We are safe, dear father!" he whispered quietly, taking the hand of Mr. Vale. "Have no fears! No one has seen us but Murlick, and I think I've settled him for the present!"

Mr. Vale did take courage at these words, and pressed the hand of his son in grateful love.

Capt. Willis and Eugene each seized an oar and paddled the raft away from the *Alabama*. They had not proceeded far when they heard sounds of confusion, and knew that the insensible body of Murlick had been discovered, or that the villain had recovered his senses and raised an alarm.

"We are detected!" said Eugene.

"And just as we were getting started, too!" responded Mr. Vale. "My God! they are getting out the boats, and will scour the waters all around the steamer! We are sure to be recaptured—we are lost!"

CHAPTER XV.

AFLOAT AND ASHORE.

The apprehension of Mr. Vale was not realized.

The sounds of alarm he had heard suddenly died out.

"They have found Murlick and are taking him to the cabin," said Capt. Willis. "Possibly they will not get at the secret of his unconsciousness under several minutes."

The new-found son and Ned continued to paddle the raft, while Mr. Vale and Ethel, recovering their calmness, busied themselves in blowing up an additional quantity of the gutta percha floats. In a hush of anxiety, yet thrilling with hope, they all toiled industriously fifteen or twenty minutes, their hearts every instant growing lighter and lighter, and at length Capt. Willis said:

"Well, we are out of sight from the steamer, and a pursuit from all her boats would not be certain to result in our capture. Thank heaven for this mercy!"

The grateful expression was echoed in the soul of each listener.

The darkness and despair in which the father and daughter and our hero had been only made their transfer to hopeful circumstances all the more thrilling.

Eugene and Capt. Willis finally ceased rowing, the former remarking:

"I think we are safe. Lost to the view of our enemies, as we now are, it's like looking for a grain of saw-dust in a mill-pond to find us! Let us rejoice!"

The hurried greetings which had taken place aboard the *Alabama* between these re-united relatives were now succeeded by more full and hearty expressions of joy and affection.

"Now that we are nearly freed from our terrible anxieties, my son," said Mr. Vale, taking the hand of the youth, "tell me all about yourself, how you came to be so well-educated, how Murlick has treated you during all these years, and how you came to be on board the *Alabama*!"

The youth seated himself nearer his father, and began relating his history as already recorded.

Capt. Willis drew his betrothed to his breast and whispered in her ears all the loving things his great and absorbing affection for her, as well as the occasion prompted.

In this blissful communion, floating on over the smooth seas, and under the starry sky, the hours wore on.

"And now we must put these floats under the boards," said Eugene, when his explanations were all made, and he and his father had entered into a perfect understanding with each other. "It will form a securer flooring for us."

Capt. Willis lent his assistance, and the task was performed, the raft then being strengthened and floating higher out of the water.

"How long are our provisions likely to last?" asked Mr. Vale, when they were again comfortably seated. "How much did you bring, Eugene?"

"The keg of water, and a cask of sea biscuit," was the reply, "besides pepper and salt enough to last us a week."

There was certainly nothing to fear immediately on the score of starvation, and Mr. Vale dismissed his fears.

"I having had more advantages than the rest of you for knowing our whereabouts," said Eugene, "will be the navigator of the party. We are well up towards the Mozambique Channel, and I think we are near the Koolin Islands. We had better make for them and conceal ourselves till the hunt for us is past!"

This proposition, meeting with approval from the entire party, Eugene shaped their course in the direction in which he supposed the group of islands he had mentioned to lie.

Hearing and seeing nothing of any pursuers, they became hopeful of a complete escape, and after talking a long time gave themselves up to fitful slumbers.

The morning broke in beauty over the waters, gilding the east with glowing splendors, and as the sun arose, the water reflecting its beams, they found themselves alone on the face of the ocean.

"See!" cried Ethel, starting from her slumbers in her lover's arms, and looking around her in delight. "The *Alabama* is not in sight!"

Mr. Vale lifted his head from his son's shoulder and echoed her joy.

"Then we are safe!" said Capt. Willis. "They may look in every direction for us, but it will be difficult for them to find us!"

There was a scene of rejoicing, in which every face glowed with joy. and every one breathed freely.

And then Mr. Vale again regarded his son intently.

In the clear morning light, he marked the honest, frank

face of the youth, and realized that he was indeed noble and good.

"This moment repays me for all my years of sorrow," he said, in a faltering voice, "and our late troubles sink into nothing in comparison with this great joy of finding my son! What unexpected happiness to know that he has not been forced into vice, as I had feared—that he is pure-minded, affectionate and imbued with lofty principles—that he is all I could desire! The great horror of our long separation is lost forever in the bliss of our re-union!"

There were tears in the youth's eyes as he embraced his father, and Ethel and her lover shared their emotion.

"And now," said Capt. Willis, when they were all restored to calmness, "let us have breakfast!"

Eugene assisted him to open the kegs and passed around his hands filled with sea-biscuit.

"This is certainly a comfortable meal," remarked Captain Willis, "and I enjoy it more than any I have eaten in the last two weeks, not excepting those on the bark after we took it! This is a nice way of life, too—for a change," he added, pleasantly, "but I hardly think I'd like it the year 'round!"

After the general laugh that followed, Ethel said:

"Why, Eugene, what is this blanket rolled around these oars for on the end of the raft? Was it intended to use?"

"Oh!" exclaimed young Vale. "I had entirely forgotten that blanket! Perhaps, however, none of us suffered from the want of it the last night. This is the use for which I intended it!"

As he spoke, he unrolled it and handed a couple of the oars to Capt. Willis, and took the others to the further end of the raft where he fixed them upright.

Capt. Willis caught his idea and erected the others in a similar manner.

The two young men then stretched the blanket and fastened it to the top of the oars, forming a convenient and comfortable awning.

"There!" said Eugene, as he again seated himself. "That

from being sun-struck. Second, it will keep our keg of water from boiling. Third, it will do for a sail and help us along in the way we desire, the wind being all right!"

His forethought was applauded, and he and Capt. Willis picked up their oars and resumed rowing.

"How bright the water is!" said Ethel, looking out upon the broad expanse around them. "Oh, Ned, what are those little white caps to the north of us?"

"That is where a school of fish are coming up to breath!" replied her lover.

"I should think they'd be astonished by our unwieldy and singular conveyance," laughed Ethel. "Perhaps, though, they think it's Neptune's car! If we had any way to cook them," she added, "I would bend a pin and catch a few!"

Her remark was met with laughter.

Mr. Vale looked at his daughter with all a father's pride, as leaning against her lover, who was steadily pulling at his oar and yet regarding her admiringly, she flung off all care and endeavored to cheer her friends. Her eyes were luminous with a clear and steady light, her hair was flung carelessly back from her brow, and her usually pale face was flushed with joy and happiness. A great change for the better had been wrought in her appearance.

"It won't do any good for us to mope and be half-dead with fear," she said. "To have good fortune, we must deserve it! We must be hopeful and look on the bright side. Oh!" She added, "just see those beautiful gulls!"

Her cheerfulness was infectious.

The brother and sister speedily became acquainted with each other, on terms of unusual fraternal affection.

Eugene and Capt. Willis continued paddling to the North, the former thinking it advisable to reach the Koolin islands, if they were really near them.

Ethel exerted herself to entertain her friends, singing to them in a low sweet voice pretty songs and ballads, and entertaining them with funny anecdotes and such scraps of oddities as happened to recur to her memory.

When the sun was in the mid-heavens, Capt. Willis dealt out their dinner of water and sea biscuits, and said:

"With a slight exercise of your imaginations, this water will pass for tea!"

"Oh," added the girl, with a laugh, as she noticed its brackish appearance, "add some of brother's salt and pepper, and it will pass for soup!"

They went on all day without meeting any ships, although they kept a look-out for them, and as the afternoon deepened, the sun half way down to the Western horizon, Eugene said, in a disappointed tone:

"I must have been mistaken. We must have been farther from the islands than I thought! It seems that we are likely to spend another night on the waters!"

"It might be in worse company," returned Ethel, archly.

Capt. Willis was looking earnestly to the North, and now exclaimed:

"See that brownish tint on the horizon, Eugene! It is the islands!"

They all looked and soon distinguished the line referred to.

The men redoubled their exertions, and, to their great delight, were soon in full view of the islands—a small, low group of limited extent and uninhabited.

"We stopped here once for water," said Eugene, as he looked shorewards. "They would never think of looking for us here! We have indeed cause for rejoicing!"

They soon reached the land and disembarked. The raft was carried ashore, and they then looked around them.

They found themselves on the largest island of the group, which comprised ten or a dozen—and in the midst of wild and delightful scenery. The island was nearly a square mile in extent, and covered with bamboo and palm trees, some of them forty feet in height. There were rocks and hills and valleys, testifying to the volcanic origin of the group, and little bays and harbors along the shores.

"The first thing to be done is to get a house!" remarked Capt. Willis, when they had fully exercised their limbs and exulted sufficiently in their good fortune. "Ethel, if you and Mr. Vale will sit down on that rock, Eugene and I will soon show you a palatial residence!"

"Wait a moment. Ned," said the merchant, seating himself with his daughter. "You know you are my son as well as Eugene—so call me father! I don't like to hear you say Mr. Vale!"

A flush of feeling appeared on Ned's face, and Ethel blushed, as her lover warmly expressed his thanks for the kind affection that had prompted Mr. Vale's remark.

The young men went to work, removing their coats, and in the course of an hour had produced a neat bamboo structure, with thatched roof, and as portable as a tent.

A bamboo screen was then made to divide the hut into two apartments, thus giving Ethel a room to herself.

When their work had been sufficiently admired, Ned said smilingly:

"Now, darling, if you'll bend a pin, perhaps we can catch one of those fish you wanted. I see the tide is out," he added. "We'll be very likely to find oysters here!"

On examination, he and Eugene discovered that there were a plenty of the bivalves within easy reach, and then brought a large quantity of them ashore.

While they were thus engaged, Ethel had gone on a scouting expedition and soon returned with some fruit shaped much like a cocoa-nut, which she declared had grown on a tree over forty feet high.

"Oh, that is bread-fruit!" said Capt. Willis. "I'll cut it in slices and show you how to bake it for supper!"

"And I found this!" said the maiden, holding up an enormous oyster shell. "Did you ever see such a monster?" It will hold as much as an ordinary tea-kettle!"

"It will do for that purpose!" said Eugene. "Let us go inland a little way and build a fire where it won't attract notice, should our pursuers come in this direction!"

They found a secluded valley in the interior, in the vicinity of which bubbled up a clear spring of water, and here they kindled a fire and cooked their oysters in the huge shell, and baked their bread-fruit in the ashes.

"This is a feast for an epicure!" said Ethel surveying the dinner she had cooked with the aid of the two young men." Stewed oysters, oysters roasted in the shell, and oysters raw; bread 'raised' and kneaded by old dame Nature herself; plenty of cool and fresh water and shells to drink it from, and hearts to enjoy it? Come, father," she added, placing a stone at one side of the fire." "I want your opinion on the capacity of our under-cooks."

Mr. Vale took his seat by the fire and did full justice to the dainty viands, declaring them delicious, and congratulating the laughing young men on their proficiency in the culinary art.

After supper the party strolled along the shore, gazing with breathless admiration at the glories of the setting sun and exploring fully the island.

Their present situation was so infinitely preferable to their close and terrible captivity on board the pirate-setamer, that they rejoiced in their freedom and happiness, not even repining for home.

In the soft moonlight, late in the evening, when sea and land were flooded in a holy beauty, the little party sat hand in hand on the rocks, listening to the beating of the waves upon the shore in low music, and talking earnestly and lovingly to each other.

At length they broke the chain of fascination that held them down by the shore, breathing in the spice-laden air, and retired to the hut, where they soon fell asleep.

The next day and the next were repetitions of the first afternoon, passing like a delicious dream. They gathered wild flowers of such beautiful forms and rare adors as were bewildering to people brought up among the sturdier plants of a temperate clime, and revelled in every form of floral beauty.

On the afternoon of the third day they were roaming inland, laden with fruits and flowers, and at length sat down to rest.

"It seems too bright to last!" sighed Ethel, on whose sweet face was the clear glow of happiness and health. I shall hate to leave this spot! It is here where we learned to love you so dearly, brother; here where father has renewed his youth and learned to laugh as gleefully as any of us; and here where we have tasted the sweets of tropical life without finding any thorns! I have felt so relieved at being away from our enemies that until now I have not given a thought to the future. When are we going to leave this sunny spot, dear Ned?"

"I have waited until all pursuit should be over," returned her lover, "before making any proposition on the subject. We had better wait here a week longer, and then form our plans. Don't you think so, father?"

Mr. Vale assented, and Eugene approved of the idea, and they soon strolled back to the shore, seating themselves on their favorite rock.

Suddenly Ethel turned deadly pale and pointed seaward.

Looking in the direction indicated, the party beheld a steamer approaching.

Full of alarm and excitement, they hastened into the densest thicket on the island.

The steamer continued to advance rapidly, and was soon near enough for them to recognize her.

She was the *Alabama*.

Continuing to watch her, they finally beheld Murlick on her deck, glass in hand.

They watched her and him in speechless anxiety until the steamer anchored near the island, and then, with a suitable sense of their peril, they asked one another how they should meet it.

CHAPTER XVI.

FURTHER DEPREDATIONS OF THE "ALABAMA."

As suspected by the fugitives, Murlick had been found insensible on the deck of the *Alabama* soon after their departure, and a great tumult had followed.

What was the secret in the case?

The subordinate officer before mentioned, stated that he had seen Midshipman Murlick and some of the men launching a raft, or something of the kind, and that he had notified Lieut. Murlick of the irregularity and singularity of his son's conduct, whereupon the lieutenant had rushed upon deck, with the result they all saw before them.

Capt. Semmes was speedily summoned to the scene, and instituted a close inquiry into the whole matter.

He found that the midshipman and Miss Vale were both missing, and promptly experienced a conviction that they had fled on a raft.

He ordered out the boats, and had the surrounding waters thoroughly explored, but obtained no trace of the fugitives.

In the meantime, he and several of his officers, including the surgeon of the vessel, gave the injured man every attention.

He was quite seriously injured, and no one wished to believe that the midshipman had made such an assault upon his superior officer and father.

Murlick finally gave signs of returning consciousness, and a continuation of the good offices of his friends was eventually rewarded by the opening of his eyes.

The baffled villain instantly commenced swearing and cursing in a manner fearful to witness.

He painted young Vale as a fiend incarnate to whose delinquenceis and villainies he had long extended the charity of silence, hoping for his reform.

He mentioned none of the real facts in the case, beyond the flight of the girl, the nature of his injury, etc., continuing to speak of Eugene as his son, and saying nothing of the presence of Mr. Vale and Capt. Willis.

Having raved an hour or two in public, and made another search around the steamer, Murlick retired to his state-room to indulge in secret the rage and disappointment which pervaded his whole being.

The following morning he proposed to Capt. Semmes to scour the neighborhood thoroughly, which was done.

They saw nothing of the fugitives, of course, but they did encounter an American ship, of which they took possession, in their usual manner.

Again, as night came, the ocean was lighted up by the flames of the ship-burners, but the decoy did not bring any additional victims.

"We may as well burn our prizes on the spot where we find them," observed Capt. Semmes to a group of his officers, as the charred hull disappeared beneath the waves. "Our dodge of saving them until night, to attract other vessels, don't pay us for our trouble. The Yankees are getting too wise to come near our burning beacons!"

The *Alabama* lay quiet the remainder of the night, to save her coal, but steamed up the following morning, and was not long in encountering and capturing an American bark, which was burnt on the spot, after the removal of her crew and a few desired portions of her cargo.

"This is the way to do it," was Murlick's bitter comment on the destruction of the vessel, as he watched the ravages of the flames. "A few such sights as this would put me into good humor. If the infernal Yankees ever do capture us, let them follow us by the track of fire which we leave behind us!"

As the *Alabama* stood away from the burning bark a thought struck Murlick, which he hastened to reveal to Capt. Semmes.

"As my son had just been figuring up the ship's reckoning, and know where we were," he said, "it is quite probable that he has shaped his course, by the aid of the stars and sun, to the Koolin islands."

"I have thought of that already," replied Semmes, "but did not care to be over-officious in the pursuit of the fugitive, you being his father."

"Never mind the relationship between us," rejoined Murlick, with an emphasis that was anything but fatherly. "As a parent I could forgive him, but as an officer I must insist on his punishment. If he is not brought to an account for this high-handed outrage, then farewell to all discipline and order!"

Capt. Semmes was entirely of this opinion, but said that he should leave the whole matter of the Court-Martial and punishment to the injured parent's direction and discretion, it being such an unusual case.

The dark eyes of Murlick gleamed savagely at this assurance, and his fingers worked convulsively. After expressing his thanks for the consideration shown him, he continued.

"I do not intend that the natural feeling of a father shall stand between the offender and his just dues. The first point is to catch him, of course, and this is the point I am coming to. You were intending to call at the Koolin islands in a few days, to see if any of the new steamers are awaiting us there, and I accordingly propose that we proceed thither at once. One of the expected vessels may have arrived a little in advance of its time, and it is quite possible that we should find her ahead of us, even if we start now. Be that as it may, the distance is not far, and the harm and inconvenience will not kill us, however the case stands!"

This was an elaborate speech for Murlick to make, and Capt. Semmes was not a little surprised at the evident desire of his subordinate to gain his approbation to the proposed measure. Wondering at the vindictiveness of his lieutenant, he replied:

"You can do just as you please, Murlick. If you really think that your son has taken refuge at the islands, you are quite at liberty to pursue him there, whether the reinforcements have arrived or not. Take your own course!"

Again a hot flash of gratified malice passed over Murlick's face, and his voice was husky with suppressed malignancy, as he thanked the captain, and proceeded to give the necessary orders for changing the course of the steamer towards the rendezvous he had mentioned.

CHAPTER XVII.

MURLICK PROMOTED AND OTHERWISE FAVORED.

The *Alabama* had scarcely dropped anchor at the Koolin islands, as already narrated, when a second steamer was seen approaching them from the southwest, and the eyes of Capt. Semmes and his lieutenant were attracted to the new-comer. The faces of the two men instantly lighted up with joy.

"We're just in time, it seems," said Murlick, "as I hoped and expected. There's one of our new war steamers, and she comes like the wind!"

Capt. Semmes regarded the approaching vessel long and steadily through his best glass,. and appeared to be a little puzzled by it.

"She's not eqactly what I expected," he muttered, "and I oan tell you before hand that she is not one of those vessels we have negociated for in England. Perhaps she is a fed, who has come this way by chance!"

For a moment the observors were filled with doubts of the new-comers character, but the signt of a Confederate flag, which was soon rnn up by her, dismissed these emotions, and caused the officers and crew the most unbounded joy.

"There's our long-promised re-enforcement," exclaimed Murlick, as he turned his glasses towards the shore, "and now, if I could see any sign of the fugitives, my joy would be complete!"

The glass suddenly fell from his hands.

He had seen the raft of the fugitives, lying on the shore!

He fairly raved in his delight.

"They are there as sure as fate!" he exclaimed, picking up his glass and handing it to Semmes. "See! There is their raft! I will order some men ashore instantly, and so prevent any possibility of their escape!"

Semmes wondered at the wild and vindictive joy of his lieutenant, and at the singular lack of paternal affection towards the young midshipman.

While he was examining the shore with the glass, Murlick ordered out a boat and sent a party of men ashore to secure it.

It was brought off and examined with many comments from both officers and crew.

"It will now be impossible for them to leave the island!" said Murlick. "They are walled in and waiting for us! We've fairly tracked 'em here, and now all that remains to do is to go ashore and take 'em!"

Semmes did not reply, and Murlick continued:

"As soon as we've greeted the new-comers, we'll scour the islands, and I'll risk but what we'll find 'em!"

Still wondering at the singular ferocity of the lieutenant, Capt. Semmes responded:

"Perhaps they've gone already!"

"Gone?" howled Murlick, looking as if the verification of the suggestion would kill him.

"Yes. The raft brought them here, but they have probably been taken off by some boat or vessel, and left it behind them!"

A look of appalling blackness appeared on Murlick's face. He could not put off his proposed hunt another moment. Muttering to himself, he hastened to dispatch a boat's crew to the shore, with orders to search every nook on the island. He would have accompanied the men himself, if the strange steamer had not been so near. In a few moments more, it was anchored alongside the *Alabama*.

She proved to be *The Scourge of the Ocean*, a Confederate vessel that had run the blockade at Mobile, with orders to look for Semmes, at this retreat, provided he was not to be found at the Cape. Her commander came on board the *Alabama*, and greeted its captain.

"I bring a captain's commission to Lieut. Murlick," said the new-comer, bowing to the villain, and handing him a package of papers. "He is to take command of *The Scourge of the Ocean*, under those documents!"

A flush of gratified ambition appeared on Murlick's dark visage as he took the papers offered him.

Semmes congratulated him on his promotion, assuring him that it was deserved, and that he felt great pleasure in seeing his merits recognized by the government.

At the head of his fellow-officers, the new commander of *The Scourge* went on board of her, and entered into formal possession.

With an exultant feeling he examined her capacity, and discovered that she was a large but ordinary steamer, which had formerly plied between Mobile and New York.

In his joy and excitement, Murlick forgot his prisoners.

He ordered wine, of which there was a small supply on board, and entertained his guests with usual sociability, offering toasts to the confederate government, Capt. Semmes, and everybody who had more or less assisted his promotion.

His late commander brought him back to business, saying:—

"Well, Capt. Murlick, again congratulating you on your deserved promotion, I beg you to relieve me of my prisoners, as you are not clogged up with a dozen cargoes!"

With a sudden flash in his eyes, Murlick testified his willingness to take them.

"Among these prisoners," pursued Semmes, "you can include those you are about to take on this island—if you can find them! As to the court martial of midshipmen, Murlick, and all that, you have full authority to act in the premises, and will oblige me by relieving me of the whole matter!"

How the eyes of the listener gleamed!

Bowing assent, he led the way to the deck, where his guests soon took their leave of him.

He then called up his subordinate officers and crew, and made a speech to them, ending it with a declaration of the mutual service required at their hands.

He then ordered out a couple of boats, selected out a score of men to man them, and started for the shore of the island.

CHAPTER XVIII.

THE CAPTOR AND HIS PREY.

The fugitives had watched all these proceedings, as far as they could see them, with feelings akin to despair.

They knew that the island did not afford any spot which, in case of a general search, could long conceal them.

On the other hand, they knew that they could not leave it, in the face of all their enemies, until after night fall.

Horrible situation!

They were soon driven out of the thicket in which they had taken refuge, on discovering the approach of the steamer, the boat's crew, Murlick had sent ashore, having gone in the very direction of this spot.

Hunted from thicket to thicket, and driven to and fro, the three men managed for a time to avoid the observation of their enemies.

They kept Ethel with them, now assisting her steps, and now carrying her in their arms.

Narrower and narrower became the limits in which they moved, a line of Confederates stretching across the whole island, and gradually sweeping the fugitives towards the sea.

It soon became evident to them that they could not much longer escape observation, yet how they struggled to do so!

The thickets from which they were dislodged, one after another, grew thinner and less frequent, and at length, just as Murlick landed at the head of his men, the weary and despairing victims were seen by their hunters.

What shouts of infernal rejoicings arose at the sight!

How quickly Murlick and his men joined in the hue and cry!

There is no necessity of lingering upon the scene.

Panting—helpless—overpowered by numbers—the three men did all that men could do, but they were secured and bound.

Murlick fairly raved in his delight, addressing himself to Ethel, then to the father and son, and finally to Capt. Willis, mocking them all with the result of their flight.

In half an hour the men were stowed away in irons the hold of *The Scourge*, and Ethel was a close prisoner in one of the state-rooms of the steamer. Their sufferings can be imagined.

The Confederates remained at the islands over night, carousing and rejoicing.

Early in the morning, a ship which had come by this out of-the way route to avoid the pirates was seized, and all the prisoners were put aboard of her and told that they could make their way to any port they pleased. The Vales and Capt. Willis were not included among these prisoners, but were retained on board *The Scourge*.

Immediately after this event, Capt. Semmes held an interview with his late lieutenant.

It was agreed that both vessels should start immediately for the Bay of Bengal, the *Alabama* making a circuit towards Java Head, and *The Scourge* beating up the mail route thoroughly, and both finally coming together again at Madras.

With this understanding, adieus were lettered by the officers of the two steamers, and each stood away on its course.

The succeeding afternoon Capt. Murlick captured an American vessel, the ship *Senator*, of New York, Capt. Joyce.

The captain, always a nervous and excitable man, had been a prey to the most harassing fears of the Confederate pirates, ever since leaving Calcutta, and at the discovery that he was really assai'ed by one of these long dreaded enemies, his mind had entirely lost its balance.

His mate, an intelligent young man, quietly surrendered the ship to Murlick, there being no help for it, and the crew was placed in the hold of *The Scourge*.

Seeing that the maniac captain was unusually quiet, Murlick conceived the idea that he was perfectly harmless, and allowed him to wander about the steamer as he pleased.

As night approached, Murlick appeared in unusually good spirits, as was natural, judging his situation from his own point of view.

His first prize had proved exceedingly valuable.

Immense piles of rich silks and shawls, etc., including every variety of East-Indian goods, had been taken out of her, and were filling his cabin and deck to overflowing.

And, better than these material gains, he had in his custody those whom he most hated, and her for whom he had conceived such a fierce and maddening passion.

"This night shall see all my annoyances swept from my path," he said to himself, as he finished plundering the ship. "Ha! ha! my life-long revenge upon the hated family of Vale will soon be completed!"

He drank deeply and blustered about, looking and acting like a fiend.

The few elements of decency and humanity that had been retained in his nature by his awe of Capt. Semmes, had all vanished since the moment of their separation, and he stood unmasked in all his moral deformity—as heartless and merciless as any common pirate that ever scoured the ocean.

As twilight deepened over the scene, he called into the cabin a couple creatures of his will, and told them to bind Capt. Willis hand and foot and put him into a bag, and then convey him to a boat alongside, taking care to avoid the notice of the rest of the crew.

This order was executed.

As fortune would have it, Ned—thus tied up in a stout coffee sack—was conveyed from his close quarters to the boat without being particularly noticed. He thought, of course, that his last hour had come.

Saying to his executive officer that he and a couple of his men would fire the ship, Murlick hastened to the boat and pushed off, and was soon aboard of the ship, which had a short time previously been cast off from the Steamer.

Our hero was lifted to the deck, half suffocated in the close sack, and conveyed to the cabin.

"I am going to leave him here," Murlick then remarked to his minions. "He has made me considerable trouble, "and I am going to get rid of him!"

The villains manifested some horrors as hardened as they were, but a feeling of curiosity succeeded, and a few inflammatory words about the Yankees, made them eager for the deed.

"Remember, I shall give you three hundred dollars apiece if you keep your own counsel," said Murlick. "Look out for him now and see that he does not make us trouble!"

Ned was taken from the sack and extended upon the heavy table in the centre of the cabin. Despite his desperate struggles, he was bound to it with a multitude of cords, so that he could not move hand or foot, and Murlick then said:

"Good night, Capt. Willis. I will tell Miss Vale where you are, and give her a chance to save your life, but do not think it hard if she should leave you to your fate!"

He turned away, arranged the combustibles for the destruction of the ship, fired them, and then went back to his steamer.

His first movement was to bring Mr. Vale and Eugene on deck, with their hands tied behind them, and set them afloat on a rude raft, with a mocking adieu, as they drifted away from the steamer.

He next brought Ethel on deck, and tied her to a gun-carriage, telling her what he had done with her lover, and assuring her that he would release him if she would promise to be his wife. Her reply can be foreseen.

After parlying with her a few minutes, he turned away in a sullen fit of wrath, and left her to herself.

"To be burnt alive in the ship!" murmured. "O, God! Will thou permit it?"

Her brain seemed reeling.

At this juncture she noticed the maniac captain hurrying across the deck near her, hatless and with his hair flying wildly about his face, appearing to her like a terrible apparition.

The mood of the madman had changed.

He had caught a glimpse of the fire breaking out on his vessel, and the sight had excited him to the highest pitch of frensy.

Before Ethel could move or speak, he had thrown himself into the boat used by Capt. Murlick, and was rowing swiftly towards the burning vessel?

CHAPTER XIX.

AN UNEXPECTED CATASTROPHE—CONCLUSION.

The situation of our hero, as the flames of the burning vessel leaped up around him, crackling and roaring, was appalling.

To die thus was horrible!

He struggled frantically with his bonds, but they only cut deeper and deeper into the smarting flesh.

"Oh, Ethel!" he moaned, the thought of her adding unmeasured horror to his anguish.

Again and again he struggled with all his strength, at the

ropes that confined him, but at length the conviction forced itself upon him that it was of no use—that, so far as his own exertions were concerned, he was doomed!

The hot breath of the fire fanned his cheek already, and his frenzied imagination saw fiery shapes flitting before him, and heard hissing sounds which he knew only too well was the approach of the devouring element.

But in this awful peril, he thought more of his betrothed than of himself.

He groaned in his torturing anguish.

And then, as his brain reeled and he would have shrieked, he heard the cabin door open, and saw a man enter.

He was the maniac captain of the ship.

"What! Are you shut up here to die?" he cried, as he rushed towards our hero. "What fiend has left you to be burned alive! We'll see! We'll see who'll be burned!"

Muttering incoherently, he flourished a huge knife around Capt. Willis, deftly cutting his bonds, and the next instant the prisoner was free!

"Follow me!" then said the madman, rushing through the flames and smoke to the door. "Hurry!"

Ned hastened after him to the deck.

The flames of the ship had risen like a wall of fire, and were driven by the wind towards the steamer, so that the motions of the two men were not seen.

"Here!" said Capt. Joyce, as he rushed to the side of the vessel.

"Jump in!"

They sprang into the boat, and the maniac then said:—

"These flames hide us from our enemies. We must go to the windward and get beyond this light, and then row in the darkness to the steamer!"

As he spoke, he pulled rapidly from the burning vessel, cunningly taking care to keep its glare between him and the confederates until he had reached the darkness outside, and then he rowed in a semi-circle towards the steamer.

The man looked wild and strange, but despite his madness, he looked to Ned like an angel of mercy!

"The crew are all busy, looking at the burning ship," muttered Joyce, "and the fiend in command is exulting over your death! But I'll soon teach him!"

Capt. Willis was revolving a dozen plans in his mind for the rescue of his friends, when he suddenly beheld a couple of men on a raft at a little distance.

He drew his companion's attention to the fact.

"Let's pick them up!" he said to Joyce. "They're my friends!"

Matters were soon explained between them, and continued their way to the vessel.

As they passed behind the *Scourge*, Ned noticed that they had not attracted attention, and that the pirates were all on the other side of the vessel, regarding the conflagration.

Capt. Murlick had just put all of his prisoners, save Ethel, into boats, and was sending them adrift.

The madman rowed alongside, securing the boat, and then whispered:—

"Here are ropes to climb aboard. I fixed them. Now's your chance, if you want to get the girl. Be quick, for I have got my revenge to attend to. I have found out where the powder is, since I came on board, and I am going to blow 'em all up!"

Before Ned could speak, the madman climbed up the steamer's side like a cat, and glided over the bulwarks and disappeared from his view.

"I'll find Ethel, if possible!" whispered Capt. Willis. "Keep quiet till I return?"

He climbed up and hastened along the deck. That part of the vessel was deserted, and he was not noticed by the crew. He saw Murlick at the opposite end of the vessel, watching for prey.

Suddenly, to his intense joy and relief, he beheld Ethel bound to a gun-carriage at no great distance from him.

Her eyes were fixed upon the fire.

No one was near her.

Ned glided to her, touching her arm, and quickly cut her

bonds. The maiden did not utter a word as she saw him but a look of strange horror was on her face.

"Come!" he whispered, leading the way across the deck.

The maiden obeyed in a mechanical sort of way, the expression of her face unchanged.

When they had reached the side of the vessel, Ned caught up a rope and fastened it about her waist, whispering:

"My own Ethel! I am no ghost—but your veritable Ned!"

She looked up with a quick glance as he lowered her into the boat and followed, and the next instant they were clasped in each other's arms!

Eugene pushed off rowing rapidly.

"Look up, my darling!" said Ned, when she had wept the awful pressure from her brain. "Here are father and Eugene!"

The maiden uttered a cry of surprise and looked up to be pressed to her father's heart.

The young men pulled rapidly from the vessel, but had not proceeded more than half a mile when they heard sounds of a great tunnel on the steamer.

And in the midst of their fears, an awful sound burst on the air, and the steamer was blown in a thousand pieces!

Pieces of timber and iron were thrown all around them, but the active efforts of the young men soon carried them beyond the reach of these projectiles. The groans of the dying fell on their ears, mingled with shrieks and cursings and the hissing of the sea.

And then all became silent.

The fugitives were alone upon the waters!

The remainder of our story can easily be told.

Two days later the little party was picked up by a Boston vessel, homeward bound, and were taken to their native land without further adventures.

Of those on board the steamer at the time of her being blown up, not one has since been heard from. They found alike a watery grave.

The subsequent career of Capt. Semmes can be traced he the attentive reader through the daily papers. Whether he will yet be captured by the active cruisers of the U. S. Government remains to be seen.

But one thing is certain, and that is the happiness of our hero and the Vales. Immediately after their arriving at home, Ethel and Capt. Willis were married and presented with a splendid country-seat by Mr. Vale, where the whole family reside in the possession of every comfort and blessing.

THE END.

IRWIN P. BEADLE'S
TEN CENT NOVEL, No. 3.

THE PATRIOT HIGHWAYMAN:

A
TALE OF THE REVOLUTION,

BY

THE AUTHOR OF "LEAH THE FORSAKEN."

The production of such a piece as "Leah the Forsaken," is within the power of but few minds. It has been admired by Hundreds of Thousands, and has attained such a popularity as few productions can ever be expected to reach. The "Patriot Highwayman" is one of the greatest efforts of its author. The hero is one of those daring, dashing, and erratic characters that at once delight and astonish the world by the boldness and brilliancy of their exploits. The author has availed himself of his strong descriptive powers to portray the acts of this most daring of the daring spirits of the American Revolution, and introduces most of the renowned personages of that eventful period. Most of the scenes are laid in the immediate vicinity of New York. The whole story abounds in dramatic incidents, and the interest which begins with the beginning of the first chapter is admirably sustained to the end. Orders should be forwarded immediately.

IRWIN P. BEADLE & Co.,
137 WILLIAM STREET, N. Y.

H. DEXTER HAMILTON & Co., General Agents,
113 Nassau Street, N. Y.

PERSONS living in out-of-the-way places, or having any cause for preferring their books to come by mail, can subscribe by the year to our

SERIES OF TEN CENT NOVELS.

The terms, in all such cases, will be $2.50 per annum (24 numbers), in advance, we paying the postage, and sending a PREMIUM besides.

TO BE ISSUED FEBRUARY 15th.

IRWIN P. BEADLE'S
TEN CENT NOVEL No. 6.

THE
MAN-EATERS;
or, The Cannibal Queen!
A Story of Wonderful Events and Exploits in the South Pacific.

By ILLION CONSTELLANO,

AUTHOR OF "THE HUNTED UNIONIST," "THE SUN SCORPION," "THE REEF SPIDER," "THE PEARL DIVER," "THE SILVER DIGGER," &c.

*** Every one has heard more or less concerning the habits and customs of the savages of the Pacific Ocean, and every one will be thankful to Mr. CONSTELLANO for this brilliant and fascinating picture of life in those distant regions. It describes the wreck of the schooner *Petrel*, of New York, on one of the Feejee Islands, and details the subsequent adventures of the persons aboard of her among those *outre* beings. It shows how a beautiful Feejee girl fell in love with the mate of the shipwrecked vessel, and shut him up in a cave, insisting on the acceptance of her suit; how the heroine of the story was persecuted by this ferocious Amazon; how the shipwrecked seamen were fattened to be eaten; and all the particulars of *real life among the Feejees*. In a word, this book is a reliable and complete account of the "Man-Eaters," and is one of those charming pictures of rustic barbarism which delight everybody, fully verifying what Byron has asserted in the fourteenth canto of *Don Juan*

"'Tis strange, but true; for truth is always strange,
Stranger than fiction!"

N.B.—It affords us great satisfaction to be able to say that hereafter Mr. CONSTELLANO will write exclusively for us.

IRWIN P. BEADLE & Co.
PUBLISHERS,
137 William Street, New York.

H. DEXTER HAMILTON & Co., General Agents,
113 Nassau street.

www.ingramcontent.com/pod-product-compliance
Lightning Source LLC
Chambersburg PA
CBHW022144160426
43197CB00009B/1425